IT'S A
RED-LETTER
Day!

HOW THE
WORDS OF JESUS
IMPACT THE HEARTS
OF WOMEN
TODAY

Debbie Dupuy

Publishing Designs, Inc.
P.O. Box 3241
Huntsville, Alabama 35810

Publishing Designs, Inc.
P.O. Box 3241
Huntsville, Alabama 35810

Editors: Debra Wright, Peggy Coulter

Cover and page design: CrosslinCreative.net
Cover image: 123RF.com

Printed in the United States of America

Publisher's Cataloging in Publication Data

Dupuy, Debbie, 1961—

It's a Red-Letter Day / Debbie Dupuy

Twelve chapters.

ISBN 978-1-945127-02-1

1. The Gospels—Example. 2. Words of Jesus—Application. 3. Christianity—Women.

Title

248.8

CONTENTS

READ THE GOSPELS
in Forty Days!

Debbie Dupuy challenges her readers to read the Gospels through in forty days. It is easy to add another dimension to the book you are holding by following the outline on pages 157–158. Debbie displays a promotional T-shirt that says on the front, "It's a Red-Letter Day!" On the back it says, "I may not be perfect, but Jesus thinks I'm to die for!"

DEDICATION

For Jesus. Every word is for You.

For Arvy, who believed in me and
encouraged me to write this book. You
are my example of true servanthood.

And for our girls, Jenna and Anna, who
are loved with an everlasting love.

With special thanks:
To Peggy Coulter who inspired
me to pick up my pen.

ENDORSEMENTS

Debbie Dupuy brings Jesus' words to life for all of us in *It's a Red-Letter Day!* Her classes are amazing!

Debra Neal—Florence, Alabama

It's a Red-Letter Day! is a spiritual and inspirational journey that will transform how you hear Jesus' own words! Strengthen your faith with Debbie Dupuy as you examine the purpose, the emotions, the power, and the love spoken from the lips of our Savior, Jesus Christ. Debbie's overwhelming love for the Word of God, for Jesus, and for the very souls of her fellow Christians has led to this compilation of the teachings of Christ. Her deep emotional connection with the Bible, along with an amazing ability to enthusiastically enlighten Christian women is very evident within these pages.

Pam Gist—Florence, Alabama

This in-depth study brightly illuminates Jesus and His words. Debbie Dupuy, a dynamic teacher, speaker, and missionary, places the red letters under a spiritual microscope. She intensely examines, dissects, and relates them to the culture of Jesus' day, and makes application for us. This examination leaves an indelible mark on our understanding of His purpose, will, and unfathomable love, empowering Jesus' followers to grow in faith and fall deeply in love with Him.

Joanna McWilliams—Tuscumbia, Alabama

Debbie Dupuy is an extraordinary Bible teacher holding high the living Scriptures and making them plain by examples and demonstrations. I've enjoyed many of her studies: *The Shepherd's Daughter, The Shepherd and the Sheep, Finding God's Purpose for My Life,* and *Remind Me, Lord.* Imagine how excited I was to attend a preview Bible study of *It's a Red-Letter Day!* and now I am thrilled to read and study the book! Debbie motivates us to understand who God is, why we should believe who He is, the power of Jesus Christ, and how He can change our lives if we have faith. But first we have to get to know Him. In this teaching, she introduces us to our Lord and Savior. I'm confident you will gain a deeper relationship with our Father. Many blessings to you!

Sonji Sullivan—Amherst, New York

From a wonderful teacher and dynamic speaker comes a life-changing book of spiritual depth written with knowledge and love. It is easy to see Debbie Dupuy's commitment to the Lord in her book, *It's a Red-Letter Day!* To all who are seeking and searching God's purpose in your life, I highly recommend this book.

Mary Evans—Amherst, New York

This book exemplifies these red-letter words: "Do you love me? . . . Feed my sheep."

Mona Green—Florence, Alabama

You will think, you will learn, and most of all you will come away with a deeper love for Christ after this study. Debbie Dupuy's vibrancy and passionate love for our Savior are contagious. I consider it one of God's blessings that He arranged for me to be a part of learning from *It's a Red-Letter Day!*

Pat Carpenter—Florence, Alabama

Although Debbie Dupuy has not been immune to the difficulties of life, she lives the life that she writes about. She is a much-in-demand teacher, speaker, and author, utilizing a quick wit and old southern charm to share the results of her research. She spends many weeks in mission fields with her husband, helping to alleviate suffering and to bring hope through the Word of God. *It's a Red-Letter Day!* abounds in knowledge, depth, and much humor, leaving each student with an insight into Jesus never-before comprehended. Her book is easy to read and hard to put down.

Gisele Rudder—Florence, Alabama

This series of Bible lessons, *It's a Red-Letter Day!*, is most inspiring and presented with a double dose of enthusiasm. Debbie Dupuy is totally dedicated to teaching others about our Savior, Jesus Christ. You know right away that her desire is that everyone truly knows Christ and what He has done, which gives hope to all people. Because of Debbie's encouragement, I am teaching a ladies' Bible class, which has been a wonderful blessing for me. I am convinced that many will be inspired, encouraged, and blessed by this book!

Patsy Gooch—Florence, Alabama

My encounters with Debbie Dupuy never fail to leave me hungrier for the Word. Her love for the Bible is contagious! When we scheduled a ladies' day last year, it was easy for me to think of a speaker. Since then many of our ladies are anticipating this book and looking forward to reading it. I am certain that none of us will be disappointed!

Hannah Burleson—Clinton, Arkansas

Have you ever met someone and a relationship just clicked? The friendship is effortless, the laughs come easy, and the interests are all the same. When I met Debbie Dupuy fifteen years ago, we spent days discussing philosophies. Debbie has a passion for God's Word that causes her to dig deep, meditate, and share. I have heard her speak countless times, and each time I come away blessed, refreshed, and challenged. She is prepared, prayed up, and powerful, yet somehow always delivers her message in love, splashed with a precious southern accent. I look forward to the reality of *It's a Red-Letter Day!*

JJ Davenport—Sheffield, Alabama

It's a Red-Letter Day! was first presented in a series of ladies' classes by a woman with the love of Jesus just oozing from every pore—Debbie Dupuy. The classes were filled with enthusiasm and love for Jesus and for the women in class. Debbie is an encyclopedia of knowledge on the Bible because she is a diligent student of God's Word. You always leave her class knowing more about Jesus and feeling blessed! This series of lessons examines the words of Jesus in the Gospels and also refers back to the words in the Old Testament that refer to Jesus. But the emphasis of the class is the four Gospels. This series of lessons promoting Jesus' words gave me many new opportunities to examine and reflect on His words and how they changed the world—and especially how they changed me. The impact of those red-letter words is dynamic and never-ending!

Sharon South—Cloverdale, Alabama

Debbie's voracious appetite for studying and sharing God's beautiful word is contagious. This study pulled me into the true love of God and recharged me with spiritual energy and a hunger to delve deeper into the scriptures.

Pat Riner—Tuscumbia, Alabama

INTRODUCTION

 Seeing Red!

When you hear someone say "I'm seeing red," you know that person is angry. Many negative emotions and thoughts are associated with "seeing red."

The purpose of this study is for you to "see red" but in an entirely different way. I want you to see red as you've never seen it before—by studying the words of Jesus.

At our best, we as believers can become stagnant in our walk with God, and that is because we often forget the "good news," and the good news is Jesus!

Throughout each lesson, remember that Jesus is a friend of sinners, and you don't have to know everything about Him to live a life of victory. My hope is that as you read and study, you will see red as truth, love, and the power that can transform your life. I pray your view of life will become different the moment you realize that Jesus is the reason you live it. The following story illustrates the seriousness of trusting Jesus.

Tightrope, the high-wire walker, didn't play it safe. He didn't do the conventional thing or expect others to understand him. He just focused on what he did best, and in the end he asked people to trust him. As you read the following dialogue, imagine yourself in conversation with Jesus.

Tightrope could do incredible stunts. All over Paris, he performed at unbelievable heights—scary! He first walked the tightrope normally. Then he asked for a blindfold. After his blindfold trek, he added another challenging feat. He walked the tightrope blindfolded, pushing a wheelbarrow.

When an American promoter read in the newspapers about Tightrope's daring ventures, he immediately wrote to the man. "Tightrope, I've seen the pictures in my newspaper, but I don't believe they are authentic. Here is a challenge. I will cover all your expenses and pay you a substantial sum of money if you will come to my country and cross over Niagara Falls with your wheelbarrow." To the challenger's surprise, Tightrope accepted the offer.

When Tightrope signed the contract, the promoter began an extensive advertising campaign. On the appointed day, a large crowd gathered. To Tightrope's credit, he was available and ready to perform. As the drumroll began, Tightrope skillfully rolled his wheelbarrow onto the wire and took his first step toward the United States.

As suspenseful seconds turned into minutes, the crowd gazed with bated breath. Then, after a flawless performance, Tightrope rolled his wheelbarrow onto firm ground. The crowd went wild. Tightrope turned to his new business partner: "Well, Mr. Promoter, now do you believe I can do it?"

The promoter answered, "Well, of course. I saw you do it."

"No," said Tightrope, "that's not what I mean. Do you really believe I can do it?"

"Don't you hear the cheering crowd? No one can deny what happened here today. I am no longer a doubter. As an intelligent man, I must recognize your great skill."

"No, no, no," said Tightrope. "Do you believe I can do it?"

"I don't know what I could do to convince you that I believe you have performed this next-to-impossible feat," said the promoter. "My confidence in your ability is 110 percent."

"Good," said Tightrope. "Now get into the wheelbarrow, and we will further thrill the audience as I wheel you across."

─────────────●─────────────

I can feel that lump in your throat.

You see, faith in Jesus is never something just to be talked about. It is something that must be demonstrated and experienced. Following Jesus is like getting into that wheelbarrow. Paul Harvey once said, "If you don't live it, you don't believe it." That's what Jesus calls us to do as we study His words and life—to live and believe them.

Jesus wants you and me to trust Him by getting into His wheelbarrow and allowing Him to take us across life's low places on spiritual tightropes. He wants us to know who He is and what He can do to transform our lives. He wants us to awaken from a sleepy-eyed faith and live spontaneously and passionately for Him. He wants our hearts and souls to be connected to Him. For some, that's a scary thought because that commitment forces us out of our comfort zone.

Walking a tightrope cannot be done in a hit-or-miss fashion, and it becomes more intense when you throw in the Niagara Falls. If Jesus were gripping the handles of that wheelbarrow, would you get in? Are you able to surrender to Him and trust His words? If you said yes, then you will never be the same again.

Keep the following directives in mind as you search for a deeper meaning of Jesus' words:

- Step into the culture, historical background, and Jewish traditions of the first century.

- Realize the impact that Jesus had on those who followed Him.

- Accept the fact that many of Jesus' words are a fulfillment of Old Testament prophecy.

- Trust the fact that Jesus never called us to play it safe or to live half-hearted lives.

Come on, get into the Lord's wheelbarrow. You'll be amazed as you let Him prove that He can do what He said. Pull up a chair and sit at Jesus' table as we study His words. "See red" because it's going to be *A Red-Letter Day*!

—Debbie Dupuy

Jesus—
The Wonderful One

He is greater than any ruler . . .
mightier than any warrior . . .
nobler than any king . . .

wiser than any sage . . .
bigger than any kingdom . . .
better than any crown . . .

lovelier than any name . . .
worthy of worship . . .
deserving of praise.

—Roy Lessin

RED LETTERS:
How They Came to Be

LUKE 22:20

The red-letter Bible has been prepared and issued in the full conviction that it will meet the needs of the student, the worker, and the searchers after truth everywhere.[1]

—Louis Klopsch

When I think of seeing Jesus' words on paper, red seems to be the color most fitting. Red is vibrant and warm. Red is a color of excitement. And most restaurant owners know that the color red stimulates the appetite.

Red has always been a color that is associated with remembrance. For example, in Medieval times red letters were used in ecclesiastical calendars to indicate saints' days and feast days. Today many of us circle important dates on the calendar in red to remind us they are special. I can picture a calendar I used last year that has red circles all over it. In fact, there are red exclamation points, large red stars, and zig-zag lines around certain dates on my calendar. When I mark up my calendar like this, I am making sure that I don't forget something important or pressing.

Many calendars today have dates printed in red, such as holidays and important events in history. Why is that? Because they stand out. Red helps us distinguish them from other dates on the calendar. Red is the color that sets things apart.

 Why Red Letters?

Millions of people around the world read the Bible every day, yet few know why we have red-letter Bibles.

- Why was red chosen to distinguish Jesus' words from all other words in the Bible?
- Have we always had red-letter Bibles?
- Were the original manuscripts of the Bible printed with Jesus' words in red?

The answer to the last two questions is no. Red letters were first used by Louis Klopsch to emphasize Jesus' words in a printing of the New Testament in 1899.

Klopsch was the editor of *Christian Herald* magazine. It is believed that while he was writing an editorial his eyes fell upon Luke 22:20, "This cup is the new covenant in my blood, even that which is poured out for you" (ASV), and he conceived the idea to print Jesus' words in red, the color of His blood.[2]

He asked his mentor, T. DeWitt Talmage what he thought of Jesus' words printed in red ink, and Talmage replied, "It could do no harm and most certainly could do much good."

The first red-letter New Testament published in 1899 had an initial printing of sixty thousand copies which soon sold out. The first red-letter Bible followed two years later in 1901. The red-letter Bible soon became the favorite of Christians around the world.[3]

> *This cup is the new covenant in my blood, even that which is poured out for you.*

Klopsch wrote an explanatory note about his red-letter Bible:

Modern Christianity is striving zealously to draw nearer to the great Founder of the Faith. Setting aside mere human doctrines and theories regarding Him, it presses close to the Divine Presence, to gather from His own lips the definition of His mission to the world and His own revelation of the Father . . . The red-letter Bible has been prepared and issued in the full conviction that it will meet the needs of the student, the worker, and the searchers after the truth everywhere.[4]

Klopsch's goal was to get the Bible into the hands of as many people as possible. He especially wanted everyone who read the Bible to understand the Scriptures, particularly the words of Jesus. As Klopsch stated in the above quote, Jesus' own words define "His mission to the world." By printing Jesus' words in red, he gave us a clearer vision of the rest of the scriptures through the eyes of Jesus. By distinguishing Jesus' words, it gives Him pre-eminence, which is where He belongs.

▌▌ How long have red letters been used to signify important words and dates?

▌▌ What are some of the benefits of red-letter Bibles?

▌▌ What verse inspired Louis Klopsch to print Jesus' words in red?

 ## Power in the Words of Jesus

God, who at various times and in various ways spoke in time past to the fathers by the prophets, has in these last days spoken to us by His Son, whom He has appointed heir of all things, through whom also He made the worlds; who being the brightness of His glory and the express image of His person, and upholding all things by the word of His power, when He had by Himself purged our sins, sat down at the right hand of the Majesty on high (Hebrews 1:1–3).

📖 According to Hebrews 1:1, how did God speak in times past?

_____

📖 Who upholds all things by the power of His word?

_____

📖 Why are Jesus' words powerful?

_____

Jesus, according to the Hebrews writer, upholds the universe and everything in it by His words. That doesn't mean Jesus is like the mythological Atlas supporting the world on his shoulders, but that He maintains and sustains it. According to Hebrews 1:1–3, there is power in the words of Jesus. He is the express image of the Father and His words are from the Father.

Christ, the Center

Since becoming a Christian at age seventeen, I have been taught that all of Scripture points to Christ. Red letters aid us in this fact. To help you visualize this concept, imagine that three people are holding three signs. The first and last signs have arrows pointing to the middle sign which says "Jesus."

- First sign: *The Old Testament.*
- Second sign: *The Gospels—Jesus.*
- Third sign: *The Epistles.*
- Genesis through Malachi, all the books of the Old Testament, point to the coming of Christ.

- The Gospels record the events of the life of Christ on earth. Those books carry the names of their writers—Matthew, Mark, Luke, and John. Then the book of Acts is the history of the church that was established on the first Pentecost after Jesus died on the cross. That book records the acts of the apostles and the spread of Christianity. The book of Acts makes a transition from the life of Christ to the activities of the early church.

- Romans through Jude point back to Christ and teach early Christians and us how to live for Him. The book of Revelation immediately follows the Epistles. It is a book of prophecy that records events that would shortly take place and prophecies about events at the end of time.

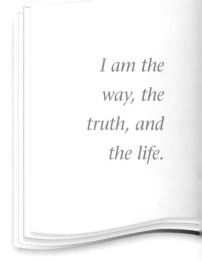

I am the way, the truth, and the life.

All Scripture harmonizes and plays to the sound of Jesus' life and death. The Bible points us to Christ and the plan of salvation that God made possible through Him, so red letters help us to harmonize and understand all of Scripture. Jesus repeatedly conveyed with His words the purpose of His coming and what He came to accomplish.

When Jesus arrived, everything changed, including the tenure of the Law. "For the law was given through Moses, but grace and truth came through Jesus Christ" (John 1:17).

Everything in the Old Testament points to the coming of Christ, and everything after the Gospels (Matthew, Mark, Luke, and John) points back to Christ. The Epistles teach us how to live the Christian life.

📖 What does Hebrews 8:7–13 teach about the Old Law?

_____

📖 What do the Gospels record?

_____

📖 What does John 1:44–45 teach concerning Jesus?

_____

📖 What do the Epistles teach us?

_____

📖 Why is 2 Timothy 3:16–17 important as we learn how to apply Scripture to our lives?

_____

📖 Why should we follow Christ's example? Live for Him? Learn of Him? Get to know Him?

_____

❤ Jesus' Words Are Life

Most assuredly, I say to you, he who hears My word and believes in Him who sent Me has everlasting life, and shall not come into judgment, but has passed from death into life (John 5:24).

Most assuredly, I say to you, if anyone keeps My word he shall never see death (John 8:51).

I am the way, the truth, and the life. No one comes to the Father except through Me (John 14:6).

The temple police made this statement about Jesus' words: "No man ever spoke like this Man!" (John 7:46). Jesus came to change lives and undo the curse of sin and shame. He came to give us a different way to live. It is through His red-letter words that we come to realize that He is who He claimed to be. Red-letter words have the power to change lives, set free the downtrodden and depressed, and help us understand that we now live under the new law of grace.

I have the deepest appreciation and gratitude for Louis Klopsch, for his reading of Jesus' words concerning His blood, and for the idea it gave him to print a translation of the Bible setting Jesus' words in red.

- Red: The color of blood that gives us life and vitality.
- Red: The color of passionate love.
- Red: The color most fitting for our Savior's words.

I must admit, red has always been my favorite color. I have loved it since childhood because it is so vibrant, but I have come to love it even more because it sets Jesus' words apart from all others. However, without Klopsch, we might never have had the opportunity to read Jesus' words in red. Because of His creativity, every day can be a "Red-Letter Day!"

To the architect, He is the chief cornerstone
(1 Peter 2:6).

To the bride, He is the bridegroom (Matthew 25:1).

To the carpenter, He is the door (John 10:9).

To the engineer, He is the new and living way
(Hebrews 10:20).

To the farmer, He is the Lord of the harvest
(Matthew 9:38).

To the gardener, He is the true vine (John 15:1).

To the jurist, He is the righteous judge (2 Timothy 4:8).

To the lawyer, He is the advocate (1 John 2:1).

To the philanthropist, He is the unspeakable gift
(2 Corinthians 9:15).

To the philosopher, He is the wisdom of God
(1 Corinthians 1:24).

To the preacher, He is the Word of God
(Revelation 19:13).

To the soldier, He is the captain of our salvation
(Hebrews 2:10).

To the statesman, He is the desire of the nations
(Haggai 2:7).

To the sinner, He is the Lamb of God that taketh away
the sins of the world (John 1:29).

—Anonymous

AN UPSIDE-DOWN SAVIOR IN A
Right-Side-Up World

JOHN 1:10–14, 16–18

But as many as received Him, to them He gave the right to become children of God.

—John 1:12

Several years ago when I began this exploration of Jesus and His words, I realized, "This is unlike any other study I have ever done." Indeed it was! As I studied the one around whom we divide time into categories of before and after Jesus' birth, something within me began to change. When I analyzed the words of Jesus with great intensity, I changed my view of Him. Jesus was not weak and passive. Quite the contrary. I discovered that His very nature runs upside down in Satan's right-side-up world. He is unlike anyone who ever lived. If you allow Him to take over your life, you will never be the same again.

On Earth and in Heaven

As He walked the earth, He was God in the flesh. In Him dwelt "all the fullness of the Godhead bodily" (Colossians 2:9). He walked and lived as we walk and live, yet He was without sin. He came to reveal the way to God through His words and example.

Jesus was acquainted with life on planet earth. He clothed Himself with flesh and dwelt among us. He spoke as a Palestinian Jew from a human larynx. He created and touched the lives of those He formed with His hands.

Jesus became a friend of sinners. That was the very reason He came down to a world of sin. He understands what it is like to suffer, face betrayal, and be misunderstood.

> He was in the world, and the world was made through Him, and the world did not know Him. He came to His own, and His own did not receive Him. But as many as received Him, to them He gave the right to become children of God, to those who believe in His name: who were born, not of blood, nor of the will of the flesh, nor of the will of man, but of God. And the Word became flesh and dwelt among us, and we beheld His glory, the glory as of the only begotten of the Father, full of grace and truth. . . . And of His fullness we have all received, and grace for grace. For the law was given through Moses, but grace and truth came through Jesus Christ. No one has seen God at any time. The only begotten Son, who is in the bosom of the Father, He has declared Him (John 1:10–14, 16–18).

> And what is the exceeding greatness of His power toward us who believe, according to the working of His mighty power which He worked in Christ when He raised Him from the dead and seated Him at His right hand in the heavenly places, far above all principality and power and might and dominion, and every name that is named, not only in this age but also in that which is to come. And He put all things under His feet, and gave Him to be head over all things to the church, which is His body, the fullness of Him who fills all in all (Ephesians 1:19–23).

> He is the image of the invisible God, the firstborn over all creation. For by Him all things were created that are in heaven and that are on earth, visible and invisible, whether thrones or dominions or

principalities or powers. All things were created through Him and for Him. And He is before all things, and in Him all things consist. And He is the head of the body, the church, who is the beginning, the firstborn from the dead, that in all things He may have the pre-eminence (Colossians 1:15–18).

Make a list of everything these verses teach you about Jesus.

_____

_____

Why are we here? What relevance does Jesus have to our faith? My fear is that we might have forgotten that in order to be a Christian, Jesus must be involved.

Jesus is the good news. If nobody knows that our good news is good, how are they going to be drawn to it?

The verses just mentioned from the pens of John and Paul are a far cry from living as a Christian who doesn't understand "what is the exceeding greatness of His power toward us who believe." Many Christians have forgotten that Jesus is the central figure of our faith. We have left Him out so we can "do church." But the church without Jesus isn't church at all.

- Who made the world? Jesus.

- Who is the image of the invisible God? Jesus.

- Who is firstborn over all creation? Jesus. ("Firstborn over all creation" means that Jesus is supreme over all the created order. He is supreme over creation because He created everything.)

- Who is before all things and by whom everything is held together? Jesus.

- Who is the head of the body, the church? Jesus.

- Who is the firstborn from the dead? Jesus.

- Who is to have first place in everything? Jesus.

23

📖 In what ways have we forgotten that Jesus must have first place in our lives?

📖 Why is He to be first according to John 1 and Colossians 1?

📖 When we talk to people about our faith, do we present the church before we present Jesus? Is it biblical to present the church first, according to the passages above?

📖 What evidence shows that He is first in your life? What steps do you need to take to make sure He is not only in first place but that He also stays there?

The Times, the Apostles, and the Places

To get a better understanding of Jesus, let's view Him through the first-century culture of Palestine. We must understand that the Jews held to the strictest form of the Old Testament law, as they knew it. They believed that the way to God was through a hierarchy based on steps toward holiness, and access to God was based on one's ancestry, a religious caste system, in effect. Race, social class, and gender were the dividing factors of the Jewish world. Even those they considered to be God's children were viewed through eyes of clean or unclean, desirable or undesirable. After all, had not God banned sinners, menstruating women, and the physically deformed from the temple?

Women in that culture were regarded as property. They were rarely taught the Torah, and were disdained if they talked to men outside their families. Women were forbidden to touch men other than their spouses. In those days, according to Jewish custom, men regularly uttered this prayer in the temple: "Blessed art thou, O Lord our God, King of the universe, who hast not made me a woman." As someone once said, "Poor you, in that culture, if you were born a Gentile, born a slave, or born a woman."

Then Jesus appeared.

 ## Jesus Is Like No Other

Jesus was a human being, a Jew in Galilee with a name and a family. At a glance, He appeared to be just like everyone else. Yet in another way He was different from anyone who had ever lived on earth.

This man had no problem associating with children, sinners, and even Samaritans. Samaritans were considered half-breeds, because they were of a mixed race. He touched and was touched by the unclean. He made His way through crowds of lepers, the deformed, and the sick. He had no problem being touched by a hemorrhaging woman or by those possessed by demons. Jesus talked freely to a woman who had five husbands, was anointed by a prostitute's oil, and traveled with a band of women throughout His ministry. He loved and valued women like no other man in that day. No wonder women were always near Him. It is not surprising that when Jesus was raised from the dead, He spoke first to a woman. That's our Jesus, the upside-down Savior in a right-side-up world.

Let her alone. Why do you trouble her? She has done a good work for Me.

Jesus turned upside down the accepted norms of His day. His actions baffled religious leaders because He did many things that could not be explained in their terms. Instead of Jesus becoming soiled with leprosy when He touched lepers, they left clean. When an immoral woman washed His feet with her tears, wiped them with her hair, and anointed them with an expensive fragrant oil, she left transformed. Jesus always preferred the company of sinners and tax collectors over the religious and pride-filled. He made sinners feel comfortable and the pious feel uncomfortable. One reason I believe sinners were so drawn to Him was that they knew they needed forgiveness. Jesus was always quick to forgive any acknowledged sin, and He still is today.

In Jesus' day, worship had become an outward display. Men prayed aloud on street corners to prove how religious they were. Today we show up, do our time, and drop money into the collection plate with little or no connection to the transforming life we can find in Jesus. If we were infected by Him, we would most certainly infect others with His transforming power. You tell me, is this happening?

📖 Do you believe we Christians have been "infected" with Jesus? Support your answer.

📖 What happens when we are truly "infected" with Jesus? Base your answer on a definition of *infected*.

📖 What actions are evident in those who are "in love" with Jesus?

📖 When Christians share the gospel, what do you expect of their regard for Jesus?

🖤 Transformed by Jesus

Today, organized religion bears little resemblance to the diverse group of social rejects and outcast as in the Gospels and the book of Acts. I think it is easy for us to lose sight of Jesus and His teachings because most of us live in middle-class America where everything is comfortable. Many people, even in the church, have this attitude: *Religion is something you do; it's not who you are.* Have we somehow lost the amazing core of Jesus' transforming life and message? I think so.

Two words one could never think of applying to the Jesus of the Gospels are *boring* and *predictable.*

> *If Jesus had never lived, we would not have been able to invent Him.*
>
> —Philip Yancey

Jesus is the Son of God, as John proclaims in his Gospel:

- He healed the sick and lame, raised the dead, walked on water, and calmed a raging storm.

- He spoke words of truth and life and fulfilled all of the Old Testament prophecies about Himself.

- He urged obedience to the Mosaic Law but was accused of being a lawbreaker.

- He bade little children to come to Him, yet He overturned tables in the Temple because of petty profiteers—twice.

- He was affected deeply by the plight of people but hated self-righteousness and pride.

What Jesus loved most was simple faith.

▐▐ Do you believe that most people think of Jesus as boring and predictable? Why or why not?

📖 Do you think of Jesus as ordinary or extraordinary? Why?

_____

📖 Make a list of some things you know about Jesus. Describe His character.

_____

_____

❤️ Picture This

When we, as believers, think of Jesus, we visualize Him as a gentle person surrounded by children. We picture Him as He is often portrayed on canvas: outstretched arms with a longing in His eyes. We picture Him as He walks across the sea, touches a leper, or sits at a well to talk to a woman whom society has scorned. We see Him as He writes in the sand.

While pictures help us visualize what Jesus could have been like, Mel Gibson's movie, *The Passion of the Christ,* compels us to see Him as the Jews saw Him. In order to understand Him and what He came to do, let's investigate the time in which He lived. Let's examine Old Testament prophecy and how He fulfilled every scripture written about Him.

Do we think of Him as passionate, emotional, or spontaneous? Perhaps not, but He was all of these things, more so, I believe, than anyone who has ever lived.

I fear we have become so accustomed to the modern-day version of Jesus that we have forgotten that He came to teach us how to live and how to know God. More importantly, Jesus came for our assurance of what true faith and vibrant life with Him can be. Do we play it safe and hide from His assurance? Philip Yancy was correct, "If Jesus had never lived, we would never have been able to invent Him." That's why He is our upside-down Savior; no one who ever lived was like Him.

BACK TO THE BASICS
with Jesus

LUKE 19:10

What other king leaves His glory; what other king leaves His throne? What other king leaves His glory to die for the sake of the world?

—adapted from Phil Wickham, Josh Farro, Jeremy Riddle

 ## Points to Remember

Today, millions around the world claim to be Jesus' followers. Famous people throughout the ages have been influenced by Him. They have quoted His words to teach and influence their students. Among them are most of the founding fathers of this nation. The list of those who have studied His teachings and claimed themselves as His followers is endless. Wherever He went and whatever He did, He changed the world.

- Jesus is the most important figure in human history. His life is so important that we have used Jesus' life on earth to divide history into two eras: before Christ (BC) and from the year of His birth (AD).

- Jesus' words have had more impact on humanity than any words ever spoken. He lived on earth only thirty-three short years, but

His example and words, two thousand years after His death, still give us life and hope.

- Jesus' recorded words were all spoken during the last three years of His life, with the exception of a brief exchange with His mother at age twelve in the Temple.

- Jesus was an itinerant rabbi who taught crowds in the fields of Galilee.

- Jesus trained disciples to be like Him.

- Jesus challenged the religious authorities of the day and confronted hypocrisy.

- Jesus calmed a raging storm by commanding it to be still. He raised the dead, fed five thousand men, and broke the shackles of sin and shame in the lives of those who encountered Him.

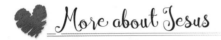 More about Jesus

The goal of this chapter is to familiarize you with the Gospel writers and to supply basic background information of the life of Jesus. To write in detail would take volumes.

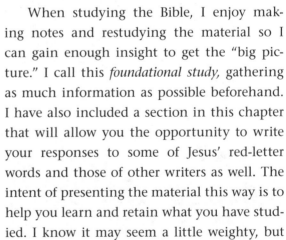

What do you want Me to do for you?

When studying the Bible, I enjoy making notes and restudying the material so I can gain enough insight to get the "big picture." I call this *foundational study,* gathering as much information as possible beforehand. I have also included a section in this chapter that will allow you the opportunity to write your responses to some of Jesus' red-letter words and those of other writers as well. The intent of presenting the material this way is to help you learn and retain what you have studied. I know it may seem a little weighty, but press through it. In order to really *know* Jesus, you first must know *about* Him.

 ## Gospel Writers

Let us begin by studying the Gospel accounts of the life of Christ. One way to do this is by comparing and contrasting the different accounts of His ministry. Read and make notes of each Gospel account of Jesus' miracles, parables, and crucifixion. Each Gospel writer approaches the event in a unique way and writes to a different audience. Assimilating the four accounts will help us complete the picture.

A further study of the life of Christ will reveal that the Gospel writers do not record the same events of His life or the miracles He performed. Jesus' life is recorded in the Gospels—Matthew, Mark, Luke, and John. These are known as the biographies of Jesus' life.

MATTHEW

❶ Matthew was a tax collector.

❷ Matthew records the genealogy of Jesus and explains that He is the fulfillment of all Old Testament prophecies about the coming Messiah (Matthew 1:1–17; 2:23; 26:56).

❸ Matthew writes to a Jewish audience and gives the path Jesus took to the cross rather than the throne. He presents Jesus as the Messiah.

MARK

❶ Mark came from a wealthy family.

❷ Mark, also known as John Mark, emphasizes Christ as the suffering Servant, the one who came not to be served but to serve and give His life a ransom for many (Mark 10:45).

3 Mark's account moves quickly and addresses a Gentile (Roman) audience, omitting things important to Jewish readers, such as genealogies, Christ's controversies with Jewish leaders, and Old Testament prophecies. Romans valued theological issues and goal-oriented people.

4 Mark portrays Jesus as a man of action and uses *immediately* as a key word. Mark often tells of something Jesus did and then reports that He immediately set out to do another task.

LUKE

1 Luke was a physician (Colossians 4:14).

2 Luke writes to a Gentile audience and refers to Jesus as the Son of Man, emphasizing His humanity. He portrays Jesus as the ideal human who was truly selfless.

3 Luke also reveals Jesus as sensitive to the poor and oppressed, and he shows that Jesus placed great value on women.

4 Luke's account is the most detailed, probably because he was a physician.

5 Luke reveals eyewitness accounts of Jesus' life (Luke 1:1–4) proving the historical accuracy and events of His life. Luke also wrote the book of Acts, giving us a historical account of the church and Jesus' ascension to the Father.

JOHN

1 John was a fisherman.

2 John, the beloved disciple, writes an up-close-and-personal Gospel account of Jesus' life.

3 His was a universal audience.

4 John's Gospel presents Jesus as the Son of God and the Savior of the world. He spells out the overall purpose for writing this account in John 20:30–31: "Jesus did many other signs in the presence of His disciples, which are not written in this book; but these are written that you may believe that Jesus is the Christ, the Son of God, and that believing you may have life in His name."

Those who are well have no need of a physician, but those who are sick.

❺ John's Gospel, more than any other, most clearly teaches the deity and pre-existence of Christ (John 1:1–2, 18; 8:58; 17:5, 24; 20:28).

❻ The book of John does not focus on the miracles, parables, and public speeches as do the other accounts.

❼ John is also the author of First, Second, and Third John and the book of Revelation.

📖 Why do we have such diversity in the Gospel writers?

_____

📖 Why is John's Gospel so different from the others?

_____

A Quick Review of Jesus' Life

❶ Jesus was born in Bethlehem, in the country of Judea (Matthew 2:1–6). Mary, His mother, had never known a man, and it was revealed to her by an angel that she was chosen by God to birth the Savior of the world. Joseph, to whom she was betrothed, had to be convinced by an angel that these things were true about her (Matthew 1:18–25).

❷ Luke records the longest account of His birth (Luke 2).

3 Jesus is called Immanuel, meaning "God with us" (Matthew 1:23).

4 When King Herod learned of Jesus' birth, he set out to destroy Him. Herod ordered all male children, age two and under, to be executed (Matthew 2:1–12, 16–18).

5 Joseph fled with his family to Egypt and remained there until the death of Herod (Matthew 2:13–15).

6 When Joseph and Mary returned from Egypt after Herod's death, they settled in Galilee in the town of Nazareth (Matthew 2:19–23; Luke 2:39–40).

7 We read of only one more thing in Jesus' life before He reached adulthood. When He was twelve years of age, He was separated from Joseph and Mary during a trip to Jerusalem to observe the Passover. They found Him in the temple talking with the teachers of the law (Luke 2:41–50).

8 Luke's account is the only record we have of Jesus' words as a youth. "Why did you seek Me? Did you not know that I must be about My Father's business?" (Luke 2:49).

9 Jesus had brothers and sisters (Matthew 13:55–56).

10 Jesus learned a trade. He was a carpenter like His earthly father, Joseph (Matthew 13:55; Mark 6:3).

11 John the Baptist baptized Jesus at age thirty in the Jordan River (Matthew 3:13–17; Mark 1:9–11; Luke 3:21–22; John 1:29–34). The Holy Spirit came upon Him and His ministry began.

12 "At about thirty years of age" Jesus came under public scrutiny and began to teach (Luke 3:23).

13 At age thirty a Jewish male who qualified could enter the temple as a priest (implied in Numbers 4:34–49).

🔢 After Jesus' baptism, He was immediately led into the wilderness to be tempted by the devil for forty days (Matthew 4:1–11; Luke 4:1–13; Mark 1:12–13).

🔢 Jesus called twelve disciples who helped Him carry out His earthly mission (Matthew 10:1–4).

🔢 Jesus' ministry began. His first miracle was turning water into wine at the wedding in Cana (John 2:1–12). He then began healing the sick, casting out demons, and teaching in the synagogues. News about Jesus spread and people began to follow Him everywhere He went.

🔢 No one had never seen or heard of such a man as this. Those of Galilee and Judea wanted to be near Him and touch Him.

🔢 Jesus' first recorded sermon was the Sermon on the Mount (Matthew 5–7).

🔢 Most scholars agree that Jesus' ministry lasted for about three years; He probably died at the age of thirty-three.

📖 Where was Jesus born?

_____

📖 Where did His family settle after they returned from Egypt?

_____

📖 What is Jesus' first recorded words? What age was He at that time?

_____

📖 How did those first recorded words reveal who He was and what He was here to do?

_____

📖 Did Jesus have brothers and sisters?

_____

📖 Approximately how old was Jesus at His baptism?

_____

📖 Where was Jesus led and by whom after His baptism?

_____

📖 What was Jesus' first miracle?

_____

📖 Discuss the basic facts of Jesus' life. Which fact is the most interesting to you and why?

_____

📖 How many years of earthly ministry do most scholars think Jesus completed?

_____

📖 At approximately what age did He die?

_____

Why Did Jesus Come to Us?

❶ "Do not think that I came to destroy the Law or the Prophets. I did not come to destroy but to fulfill" (Matthew 5:17).

📖 Why did Jesus come?

_____

❷ The Spirit of the Lord is upon Me,
Because He has anointed Me
To preach the gospel to the poor;
He has sent Me to heal the brokenhearted,
To proclaim liberty to the captives
And recovery of sight to the blind,
To set at liberty those who are oppressed **(Luke 4:18).**

📖 Why did Jesus come?

_____

❸ "The Son of Man did not come to be served, but to serve, and to give His life a ransom for many" **(Matthew 20:28).**

📖 Why did Jesus come?

_____

❹ "I have come as a light into the world, that whoever believes in Me should not abide in darkness. . . . For I did not come to judge the world but to save the world" **(John 12:46–47).**

📖 Why did Jesus come?

_____

❺ "For the Son of Man has come to seek and save that which was lost" **(Luke 19:10).**

📖 Why did Jesus come?

_____

❻ "I have not come to call the righteous, but sinners, to repentance" **(Luke 5:32).**

📖 Why did Jesus come?

_____

7 "For God did not send His Son into the world to condemn the world, but that the world through Him might be saved" (John 3:17).

📖 Why did Jesus come?

_____

📖 How does reading the words of Jesus concerning why He came help you to understand just how valuable you are to Him?

_____

📖 How is your life different because He lived? How is the world different because He came?

_____

Other Accounts of Why Jesus Came

1 "But we see Jesus, who was made a little lower than the angels, for the suffering of death crowned with glory and honor, that He, by the grace of God, might taste death for everyone" (Hebrews 2:9).

📖 Why did Jesus come?

_____

2 "He who sins is of the devil, for the devil has sinned from the beginning. For this purpose the Son of God was manifested, that He might destroy the works of the devil" (1 John 3:8).

📖 Why did Jesus come?

_____

3 "As the children have partaken of flesh and blood, He Himself likewise shared in the same, that through death He might destroy him who had the power of death, that is, the devil, and release those who through fear of death were all their lifetime subject to bondage" (Hebrews 2:14–15).

📖 Why did Jesus come?

_____

📖 What other incredible thing do we learn about Jesus and humanity?

_____

💜 Jesus' Connection to the Old Testament

Let's note some observations from different authors in the book *Jesus: A Theography* by Leonard Sweet and Frank Viola[5] which I paraphrased below. Research and comment on the added scripture references.

1 Jesus saw Himself as the manna that came down from heaven to feed Israel in the wilderness (John 6:31–58).

2 Jesus was the Lamb of God, which gave the people of God the strength to leave Egypt by eating it, and that saved them from death by shedding its blood (John 1:29, 36; 6:53–56).

3 Jesus saw Himself as greater than Solomon (Matthew 12:42).

4 Jesus was worthy of more glory than Moses (Hebrews 3:3).

5 Jesus was greater than Elijah (Luke 4:24–26).

6 Jesus saw Himself in one of Jonah's experiences (Matthew 12:40).

I am He who lives, and was dead, and behold, I am alive forevermore.

39

Jesus and Moses Compared

Pharaoh tried to kill all the Hebrew baby boys in Goshen, but Moses was saved (Exodus 1:22–2:10).	King Herod tried to kill all of the baby boys in Bethlehem, but Jesus was saved (Matthew 2:13–18).
When Moses' life in Egypt was in danger, he fled to Midian and later returned to Egypt (Exodus 2:15; 4:19–20).	When Jesus' life in Israel was in danger, Joseph and Mary took Him and fled to Egypt. They returned to Israel after King Herod died (Matthew 2:13–21).
Moses was rejected by his own people: "Who made you a prince and a judge over us?" they asked him (Exodus 2:14).	Jesus was rejected by His own people: "His own did not receive Him" (John 1:10–11).
Moses ascended a mountain to receive the Law (Exodus 19:1–3).	Jesus ascended a mountain to give a new "Law" (Matthew 5–7).
Moses was the mediator of the old covenant through animal blood (Exodus 24:1–8).	Jesus is the mediator of the new covenant through His blood (Matthew 26:28; Hebrews 12:24).
Moses fasted forty days and nights (Exodus 34:28).	Jesus fasted forty days and nights (Matthew 4:2).
Moses led the exodus of God's people from Egypt (Exodus 12:50–51).	Jesus led the new exodus, bringing people out of the world system (Colossians 1:13–14).

In a dot-to-dot book, you may have an idea of what the picture is, but you don't fully see it until the dots are connected. Then voila! The picture becomes clear. So we must connect our dots to reveal Jesus.

That's as basic as it gets.

The Impact of JESUS' WORDS AND LIFE

MATTHEW 5:12; JOHN 15:18, 20

Only in a world where faith is difficult can faith exist.

—Lee Strobel

Throughout the ages, men have been skeptical of Jesus' deity and power. For example, Lew Wallace, "one-time atheist, military general and literary genius, who along with Robert Ingersoll agreed together they would write a book that would forever destroy the myth of Christianity."[6] After two years of research to disprove Christianity, the opposite happened. Jesus' existence had a profound impact upon Wallace's life. Like the intricate weaving of a small thread through a beautiful tapestry, every detail of the knowledge about Him influenced Wallace's opinion. He stated, "It only remains to say that I did as resolved, with results—first, the book *Ben-Hur*, and second, a conviction amounting to absolute belief in God and the Divinity of Christ." In 1880, Wallace wrote the book, *Ben-Hur: A Tale of the Christ*, one of the greatest American novels ever written concerning the time of Christ.

Similarly, the late C. S. Lewis, professor at Oxford University in England, left the religion of his childhood and embraced atheism enthusiastically. Lewis was an agnostic who denied the deity of Christ for years. But he, too, in intellectual honesty, after thorough research, concluded that Jesus is God and the Savior of humanity. Over the years, Lewis wrote many books to uphold ideals of Christianity, including *The Chronicles of Narnia*, *The Most Reluctant Convert*, *The Screwtape Letters*, and *Mere Christianity*.

Lee Strobel, a known atheist and lawyer, decided to study Jesus after his wife's conversion. As an atheist, he had believed that Jesus was at best a good teacher, but later Strobel wrote the Christian classic, *The Case for Christ*. Strobel confessed that the evidence was overwhelming. His goal was to study Christ as a court case and try the evidence. When Strobel saw the evidence, he concluded that it was undeniable.

Charles H. Spurgeon once said, "There is no difficulty which Christ cannot remove, no knot which He cannot untie, no question which He cannot answer." How true that is.

THE AGNOSTIC

Several years ago, my husband, Arvy, and I met a man who claimed to be an agnostic—one who believes it is impossible to know if God exists. "John" attended worship because his girlfriend was a believer, and he wanted to make a good impression on her. But he was always quick to say, "I just don't know if God is real." As a student of scientific reasoning, John shared his belief: "There isn't enough evidence to prove that God exists, and there's certainly no proof that Jesus is the Savior of the world."

John kept attending worship. He began to listen, learn, and observe. Eventually John agreed to study the Bible with Arvy. At first he asked many questions and struggled with logical answers, but each week he returned for more and kept studying. Often after a study, Arvy told me, "I feel like

I've been through a biblical boxing match." But after several weeks, John began to soften. He began to question what he had believed.

I will never forget the day John surrendered to following Christ and to baptism. What he told my husband before he confessed Christ was heart wrenching: "All of my life I have sought answers and wondered if Jesus really existed. I could never allow myself to believe it was true. But today I am here, telling you that I want what you've got. I want the peace and assurance that only Jesus can give."

As Arvy buried John in water, God buried the old man. As Arvy raised John from the water, God raised a new man. John the agnostic had become John the believer. That was six years ago, and Arvy and I will never forget the day that John became a follower of the One and Only: Jesus!

———————————●———————————

Isn't it wonderful that Jesus can make such an impact on individuals? And it all begins by believing His words. The truth of the matter is that when anyone studies the life and words of Jesus, powerful changes are likely to take place within the heart and mind.

📖 Why do you think studying Jesus' words stirs the heart of people?

_____

📖 How do Jesus' words stir your heart?

_____

📖 Now is the time in our study for you to begin reading through the Gospels, using the reading plan on pages 157–158. Use a notebook to record interesting facts and information as you read. The only way to know the one and only Savior is to read His inspired biographies. I encourage you to do so as a class or with a friend.

The fellowship will encourage and motivate discussion in your learning process.

The Only One Worth Dying For

New Testament Christians leave us a legacy because of their deep convictions to follow Christ. When I read the accounts of the twelve apostles, I realize that they followed the Lord wholeheartedly. Their examples humble me. They stir my heart and motivate me to have deeper belief in Him.

The early Christians faced unimaginable deaths. They willingly subjected themselves to horrific circumstances. Why would they do those things if what they had seen and heard were not true? It has to be true. Every time I read about them, something within me has to step back and take a deep breath. When I read their words and examine their lives, my faith grows deeper. Maya Angelou once said, "You are the sum total of everything you've ever seen, heard, eaten, smelled, been told, forgotten—it's all there." That is precisely what it was like for those who knew Jesus.

📖 Discuss the sense of urgency of the Samaritan woman's announcement, "Come, see . . . " (John 4:29).

📖 What was the impact of her announcement and the question she asked?

📖 What application of John 4 can you make to your daily life?

Jesus Never Promised It Would Be Easy

- "Rejoice and be exceedingly glad, for great is your reward in heaven, for so they persecuted the prophets who were before you" (Matthew 5:12).

- "If the world hates you, you know it hated Me before it hated you" (John 15:18).

- "Remember the word that I said to you, 'A servant is not greater than his master.' If they persecuted Me, they will also persecute you. If they kept My word, they will keep yours also" (John 15:20).

- Great multitudes went with Him. And He turned and said to them, "If anyone comes to Me and does not hate his father and mother, wife and children, brothers and sisters, yes, and his own life also, he cannot be My disciple. And whoever does not bear his cross and come after Me cannot be My disciple. For which of you, intending to build a tower, does not sit down first and count the cost, whether he has enough to finish it—lest, after he has laid the foundation, and is not able to finish it, all who see it begin to mock him, saying, 'This man began to build and was not able to finish'? Or what king, going to make war against another king, does not sit down first and consider whether he is able with ten thousand to meet him who comes against him with twenty thousand? Or else, while the other is still a great way off, he sends a delegation and asks conditions of peace. So likewise, whoever of you does not forsake all that he has cannot be My disciple" (Luke 14:25–33).

Jesus never promised it would be easy to follow Him. In fact, at this moment Christians are meeting secretly in underground churches. Even in this modern twenty-first century, it is against the law to own a Bible in some countries. It was no different for those in the first century. Often, discipleship was punishable by death, yet they persevered.

After Peter and John had healed a man lame from birth, they were reprimanded by an assembly, which included the high priest, but they replied, "We cannot but speak the things which we have seen and heard" (Acts 4:20).

> That which was from the beginning, which we have heard, which we have seen with our eyes, which we have looked upon, and our hands have handled, concerning the Word of life—the life was manifested, and we have seen, and bear witness, and declare to you that eternal life which was with the Father and was manifested to us—that which we have seen and heard we declare to you, that you also may have fellowship with us; and truly our fellowship is with the Father and with His Son Jesus Christ (1 John 1:1–3).

📖 What do Peter and John tell us they witnessed concerning Jesus?

_____

📖 Why can we trust their words?

_____

📖 How do their words encourage your faith in Jesus?

_____

 ## Ready to Suffer

Jesus made an impact on those who encountered Him, especially the twelve apostles. He called each one of them to follow Him. Extra biblical history tells us they suffered because they believed and followed Jesus. In fact, they gave their lives because they believed in the one called Christ.

All of us have wondered how the apostles died. Many conflicting accounts of their deaths have been published. In the case of Peter's death, which some say occurred in Rome, we have no biblical record of Peter's ever being in Rome. With the exception of Judas' suicide, inspired history speaks only of James' death. Herod Agrippa, grandson of Herod the Great, killed him with a sword (Acts 12:2).

However, here are some traditions of the deaths of some of the apostles:

- Peter was crucified upside down at his request, since he did not feel worthy to die in the same manner as Christ.

- Paul was beheaded. One of the traditions is that Paul was beheaded by two messengers of Nero, as he knelt to pray.

- Thomas was speared to death.

- Matthias was said to have been stoned and then beheaded.

- Philip, according to the Roman writer Hippolytus, was crucified head down and feet up, then stoned to death.

- The death of Bartholomew was confirmed by Hippolytus of Rome. Bartholomew traveled to several counties, including India where he preached and translated the gospel of Jesus into the local language. In India, he was badly beaten, flayed alive, and crucified with his head facing downward.

- John was placed in a cauldron of boiling oil, but miraculously escaped death. He was later banished to the isle of Patmos.

- Jude was shot with arrows.[7]

In whatever manner the apostles died, we know they believed strongly in the words of Jesus and suffered much for that cause. Shouldn't you and I do the same? How do the apostle's deep convictions encourage you?

In addition to the apostles, here are examples of others who gave their lives:

- *Christians.* Emperor Nero used them as human torches.[8]

- *Polycarp.* His martyrdom was the first to be recorded in post-New Testament times. He was burned at the stake for his faith in Jesus Christ. It has been said that Polycarp was responsible for converting many from Gnosticism. Why did the Romans want to arrest him at the age of eighty-six? That's unclear, but nonetheless he did not resist when they came to his house. As his friends urged him to run, Polycarp replied, "God's will be done."

  While he was interrogated in front of a crowd of onlookers, Polycarp was unfazed, even though he was threatened with being thrown to wild beasts and burned at the stake. Polycarp told the proconsul, "Fire lasts but a little while, but the fires of judgment (reserved for the ungodly, he slyly added) cannot be quenched." He went further and said, "But why do you delay? Come, do what you will."

  It is said that he prayed aloud while the fires were lit, and his flesh was consumed.[9]

▊▊ Why did the apostles and many other first-century Christians give their lives because of their belief in Jesus?

_____

▊▊ Consider the severe torture of those who died. What does this explain about their faith and willingness to die?

_____

▊▊ Why is following Jesus difficult?

_____

▊▊ What should our commitment to Jesus cost us?

_____

♥ What Does It Cost Me?

No one else has made the impact on humanity that Jesus made. Lew Wallace, C. S. Lewis, Lee Strobel, and many others decided to weigh the evidence of Jesus' life only to find they had been wrong about Him. Many of our contemporaries who live in countries hostile toward Christianity sacrifice their lives to follow Jesus. Their faith and commitment humble me. I have to believe that Jesus has the power to change any life and touch any heart so impressionably that every true follower is willing to give everything to be His disciple.

> "Radical obedience to Christ is not easy . . . It's not comfort, not health, not wealth, and not prosperity in this world. Radical obedience to Christ risks losing all these things. But in the end, such risk finds its reward in Christ. And He is more than enough for us."[10]

♥ The Transforming Touch of Jesus

When we come to know Jesus and what He can do, we too will risk everything to follow Him. When we allow Him to touch our lives as deeply and profoundly as He touched the Twelve and so many others, there is nothing that can change our belief in Him.

A little girl proudly wore a shiny cross on a chain around her neck. One day she was approached by a man who said to her, "Little girl, don't you know that the cross Jesus died on wasn't beautiful like the one you're wearing. It was an ugly, wooden thing."

To which she replied, "I know. But they told me in Sunday school that everything Jesus touches, He changes."

Will you share with the world how Jesus touched you?

WHY BELIEVE THE WORDS OF JESUS?

1 All other religious reformers came to live; He came to die.

2 All others left memorials; He left none. No one can find His birthplace or any of His possessions.

3 All others wrote diaries and memoirs. He wrote in the sand.

4 All others chose their followers from the rich, powerful, and influential. He chose the poor and the needy.

5 All others praised human righteousness. He condemned it.

6 All others sought those who could help them. He sought those He could help.

7 All others rewarded the most talented with titles and places of honor. He taught, "If anyone desires to be first, he shall be last of all and servant of all" (Mark 9:35).

8 All others said, "Follow me and I will show you the way." He said, "I am the way, the truth, and the life" (John 14:6).

9 All others are dead, but I tell you, He is alive.

10 All others changed nothing; He changed everything.

11 All others led to a hopeless end, but life with Jesus is an endless hope.

PASS THE SALT—
Becoming a Salty Christian

MATTHEW 5:13

*And every offering of your grain offering you shall
season with salt; you shall not allow the salt of the
covenant of your God to be lacking. . . . With all your
offerings you shall offer salt.*

—Leviticus 2:13

D o you remember watching *Sesame Street* as a child?
One of the many teaching tools was to have you discover what didn't belong. Images of items that were
alike would appear on the screen. Then suddenly, a very different
image would pop up. Big Bird would say: "Can you tell which thing
is different by the time I finish this song?"

Picking out something different may seem like going back to
preschool, but Jesus' red-letter words from the Sermon on the Mount
are just that simple. We are to be different; we are salt.

You are the salt of the earth; but if the salt loses its flavor, how shall
it be seasoned? It is then good for nothing but to be thrown out
and trampled underfoot by men (Matthew 5:13).

The red letters in this passage teach us that Christians are not
to be like people in the world, those outside of Christ. Being salt
stresses our character, rather than our works. As followers of Christ,

51

we are supposed to stand out just like the preschool *Sesame Street* visual. It should be easy to pick us out in a crowd because of who we are and who we follow.

 A Different Standard

How do we do that? We begin by changing the way we think by learning His ways. Then we change the way we live and demonstrate to those around us what following Jesus looks like. Following Him means that we live by a different standard than those who don't believe in Him. And even more importantly, we understand that our hearts and minds are connected to His will. We are not followers in word only or just in faithful church attendance, but we allow Jesus to penetrate every fiber of our being. Church attendance is not done out of obligation, and our actions will certainly line up with our words. We don't follow the world's ways, feed upon the world's entertainment and lifestyles, and live with half-hearted faith. With Jesus it's all or none. There are no fence straddlers or lukewarm hearts. We can see this by what Jesus said.

The Importance of Salt in Jesus' Culture

Salt is not very exciting to us today. It is cheap and plentiful and common in our kitchen cabinets. However, it is essential to our survival, and Jesus used it to illustrate Christian living. His listeners well understood His salt metaphor that taught purpose and direction for daily living. Let's consider the history of salt in Jesus' day, along with the spiritual implication for any culture.

Salt was a main preservative in Jesus' day. It preserved their food and purified and killed germs. It was a precious substance in pre-refrigerator days. Salt also had healing powers. And finally, salt, when mixed with the bland, resulted in a palatable product.

Consider the spiritual application. As salt, we help our culture to persevere by upholding what is good in our society. We salt others and bring them into contact with the healing power of Jesus' blood. Then, as salt, we encourage new Christians to remain free from the influence of Satan and learn to recognize a dysfunctional lifestyle.

Also, Jesus' listeners knew the value of salt to the working class. In ancient Rome, soldiers were paid in a ration of salt, *salarium* (Latin), from which we derived the English word "salary." If a soldier did not perform well, it was said that he was not worth his salt. That's how precious salt was in that culture. Even those ancients knew that a good life depended on it.

It is to be thrown out and trampled underfoot.

Spiritually speaking, are you worth your salt? How are you influencing those around you? Your lifestyle and actions as a Christian are examined by those around you. Your well-being, as well as that of others, depends on how you live the "salt life." Just as the soldiers in ancient Rome depended on salt, your spiritual life depends on it.

Furthermore, Jesus taught that salt can be contaminated. His audience knew exactly what He was saying. They understood the dangers of contamination with dust, sand, or some other impurity. If polluted, salt's ability to save was diminished. Contaminated salt, Jesus said, "is good for nothing," so far as its primary usages were concerned. When salt lost its flavor, it was good for only one thing: to kill vegetation. Farmers covered their weedy fields and out-of-control grassy areas with spoiled salt. I suppose we can think of it as the ancient version of a modern-day weed killer.

How was salt contaminated in ancient times?

📖 Spiritually, how do we lose our "flavor" or influence?

_____

📖 What are two indicators that Christians are no longer "worth their salt"?

_____

❤️ *Silence Is Not Always Golden*

Jesus makes a spiritual application. When we, as followers of Christ, stop being salt, we stop influencing others for good. When we fail to speak out on issues that affect faith and family, such as abortion, homosexuality, and other moral issues, our silence has a profound negative effect on society. Our silence opens Pandora's Box. Why do we stay closed mouthed when we know others are headed for a life of misery because of their choices? Why do we turn our heads and dismiss wrongdoing, believing it's just none of our business? We all know that is not what the Bible teaches. Isaiah's ancient warning still applies to us today:

> Woe to those who call evil good, and good evil; who put darkness
> for light, and light for darkness; who put bitter for sweet, and sweet
> for bitter (Isaiah 5:20).

As Christians, we should be standard setters, examples of good, guideposts who point others in the right direction. Every society stands or falls based on the influence its constituents have on one another. We seem to have our signals wrong when it comes to living our faith and connecting to our cultural influence. For example, in a 2014 Barna Research study, forty-seven percent of adults in our country believe that marijuana should be legalized. But this same group believes that using marijuana is morally wrong.[11] Where is the disconnect? Do we understand that we should oppose what is morally wrong? If so, why then would we want to legalize what is morally wrong? We must be confused because we are saying one thing and doing another. We are inconsistent. Jesus wants us to get the connection when He teaches about the proper uses of salt. "Salty Christians" understand the link between their behavior and their belief.

■■ What was Jesus teaching when He said, "You are the salt of the earth"?

_____

■■ How can you be a salty Christian in our culture?

_____

■■ Relate this to your life spiritually. How does Christianity inspire action (James 2:12–18)?

_____

■■ How can we be standard setters in our culture without knowing what the Word of God says?

_____

♥ Did We "Okay" That?

Following the September 11, 2001, attacks, CBS interviewers of *The Early Show* asked Anne Graham Loitz, daughter of famed evangelist Billy Graham, "How could God let something like this happen?"[12] Her condensed response follows.

> I believe that God is deeply saddened by this, just as we are, but for years we've been telling God to get out of our schools, to get out of our government, and to get out of our lives. And being the gentleman that He is, I believe that He has calmly backed out. How can we expect God to give us His blessing and His protection if we demand that He leave us alone?

I think it started when Madalyn Murray O'Hair complained she didn't want any prayer in our schools, and we said okay.

Then we were forbidden to read the Bible in school, the Bible that says "thou shalt not kill," "thou shalt not steal," and "love your neighbor as yourself." And we said okay.

Then Dr. Benjamin Spock said we shouldn't spank our children when they misbehave because their little personalities would be warped and we might damage their self-esteem. So we said okay.

It became difficult for teachers and principals to discipline our children when they misbehaved. And we said okay.

Then it became socially acceptable to let our daughters have abortions if they wanted, and they didn't even have to tell their parents. And we said okay.

Then some wise school-board member advised us to give our sons all the condoms they wanted, so they could have all the fun they desired, and not tell their parents they got them at school. And we said okay.

And then the entertainment industry began to make TV shows and movies that promoted profanity, violence, and illicit sex, and music that encouraged rape, drugs, murder, suicide, and satanic themes. And we responded, "It's just entertainment, it has no adverse effect, and nobody takes it seriously anyway, so go right ahead."

Now we're asking ourselves why our children have no conscience, why they don't know right from wrong, and why it doesn't bother them to kill strangers, classmates, and themselves. Probably, if we think about it long and hard enough, we can figure it out. I think it has a great deal to do with "we reap what we sow."

▌▌ List other cultural norms to which we as Christians have said okay.

It's easy to see the cultural results of neglecting what is right. The world around us has a terrible problem: sin sickness. People live in dysfunction, hurt, brokenness, and shame all because of this disease. Christians should notice and be willing to help to change the conditions of those around them. We can show and teach them that life can be different by our examples.

 Jesus' Purpose; My Purpose

Stop and ponder: Do you remember some of the reasons Jesus said He came? As He began His ministry in His hometown of Nazareth, Jesus referenced Isaiah: "He has sent Me to heal the brokenhearted, to proclaim liberty to the captives and recovery of sight to the blind" (Luke 4:18; Isaiah 61:1–2). How do we translate that to people around us, especially those who are living in sin and dysfunction? When we think of our nation and those who have not known Jesus, we must look with spiritual eyes. In many ways, our nation has become desolate and dark spiritually, and influenced by sin. We have to understand that is what a home, a country, or a church can become if there are no salty people. Are you salty?

Salt brings out the flavor in food. When Jesus taught those listeners on the hillside, He helped them see this concept: *Just as salt flavors, we can enhance the lives of those around us.* In my simple way of thinking, it's as if the desolate, dark places become lush and green. It's like going from black and white to technicolor.

Salt has an amazing list of attributes. It has a lingering influence. It seasons, purifies, flavors, penetrates, cleanses, creates thirst, and stimulates hunger. Amazing! Now think about the properties of salt from a spiritual standpoint. We can do all of those things too.

■■ What would happen to our culture if every Christian assumed the properties of salt and its effect when put to use?

📖 Would we see a dramatic change in our homes, schools, and even our churches?

Here are a few examples of the attitudes and actions of a salty Christian:

- You are able to help a broken culture understand that sin always leads to problems, heartbreak, and devastation.
- You assume a proper role, and you're quick to influence.
- You are ready to answer questions and stimulate thirst among a world of people who need the living water that Jesus offers.
- You show love and compassion with the realization that you, too, were once sin sick and in need of help.

Oh, the difference you could make in this world if you became salty in your home, school, community, and nation.

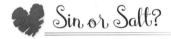 Sin or Salt?

Maybe we have forgotten how to be savory salt. Paul's life is a role model for every Christian who reads of his mighty life for Christ. He says, "Imitate me, just as I also imitate Christ" (1 Corinthians 11:1).

Paul also warned fellow Christians about their examples. Nevertheless the solid foundation of God stands, having this seal: "The Lord knows those who are His," and "Let everyone who names the name of Christ depart from iniquity" (2 Timothy 2:19).

📖 Sin is like throwing a stone in water. A ripple effect always follows. From your experiences, describe the effects of sin in this world.

📖 How would our culture change if every Christian assumed the properties of salt?

📖 Who is our example?

📖 How are we "polluted" when we fail to follow Jesus?

📖 What are we to do as His followers?

💙 Pressing on to Perfection

You may be thinking, "I'm not perfect, so how can I possibly point others to a salty lifestyle?" We will never be perfect, but when we look to the *one* who is and how He teaches us to live more perfectly, we can become what Jesus already expects us to be: Salt.

Peter encourages us in 1 Peter 2:21, "To this you were called, because Christ also suffered for us, leaving us an example, that you should follow His steps."

📖 Do we use the "I'm not perfect" plea as an excuse for not being the salt we need to be?

📖 How is our influence affected when we make excuses for our lack of growth?

📖 Take a good look at yourself and do some personal inventory. List at least two areas to challenge yourself to "press on to perfection."

_____

> Therefore gird up the loins of your mind, be sober, and rest your hope fully upon the grace that is to be brought to you at the revelation of Jesus Christ; as obedient children, not conforming yourselves to the former lusts, as in your ignorance; but as He who called you is holy, you also be holy in all your conduct, because it is written, "Be holy, for I am holy" (1 Peter 1:13–16).

📖 Why is a personal "salty" inventory more difficult than an inventory of another person's life?

_____

📖 How often should we take a personal inventory?

_____

As Peter encourages us to holy living, let's pray, using his words in 1 Peter 1:13–16 to help us:

> Lord, help me to become as an obedient child, not conforming myself to the former lust (ways and conduct), as in our ignorance, but as He who called us is holy, help me to be holy in all my conduct because it is written, "Be holy, for I am holy."
>
> Lord, help me to seek holiness above all else and become salty for You. Also help me to follow Christ's example and become more and more like Him. Lord, I know this does not mean that I become perfect, but it does mean that I can become holy and righteous because of Him. Create in me a desire to help others become thirsty for You and Your ways. Help me penetrate the lives of those around me for good and strengthen me to be a better example when I need the courage to speak up for what is right.
>
> Lord, please make me salty.

"LIGHT LIVING"—
Turn on the Light

MATTHEW 5:14–16

*There are two ways of spreading light: to be
the candle or the mirror that reflects it.*

—Edith Wharton

I grew up in Haleyville, a small town in northwest Alabama. All my life I heard the story that the first 9-1-1 call in America was made in my hometown. That call was said to have been made by a woman who hysterically blurted out: "My water just broke! Please send help!" The 9-1-1 dispatcher sent a plumber, but he later found out the woman needed a doctor. Soon after the call, she delivered her baby.

This story was spread by word of mouth. *Smithsonian Magazine* reported in February 2017 that an incident similar to the one described above did occur around 1970 in Haleyville about two years after the installation of 9-1-1. The early 9-1-1 operators were not trained, so the mix-up similar to the one above resulted.

However, the very first 9-1-1 call in America *was* made there in February 1968 when Alabama speaker of the house called from the Haleyville mayor's office to the Haleyville police station. One of Alabama's U.S. representatives answered on a bright red phone, which was on display in the lobby of the city hall.[13]

The citizens of Haleyville are proud to be the home of the first 9-1-1 call. They are quick to tell you they need the emergency system, because their area is known as Alabama's "tornado alley." Several years ago, Haleyville, along with many other small towns in the surrounding area, was devastated by a tornado. What a deeply emotional time, suffering through the loss of life and property! The area was without power for several days. There is nothing like learning to be thankful for seemingly small things when a tragedy occurs. When flipping a switch doesn't dispel the darkness, there's a quick realization that light is not a small thing!

Light is precious. If you don't believe that, try living without it a few days. I don't like living in the dark, so when the power goes off, I want to give Thomas Edison a high five for inventing the light bulb. What about you?

1 Discuss a time when you were without power. How did it feel to be in the dark?

2 Compare the discomfort caused by physical darkness to that of spiritual darkness.

 ## Oil in My Lamp

Light is a precious thing, but in Jesus' day, there were no bulbs or electricity. Their light came from a small terra-cotta bowl filled with oil that fed a burning wick. Matches had not yet been invented, so it was important to keep the light burning. Upon leaving the house, the occupants covered the light with a bowl or basket to protect the flame. Listen to Jesus' words:

> You are the light of the world. A city that is set on a hill cannot be hidden. Nor do they light a lamp and put it under a basket, but on a lampstand, and it gives light to all who are in the house. Let your light so shine before men, that they may see your good works and glorify your Father in heaven (Matthew 5:14–16).

Our mission should be to carry salvation to the ends of the earth. A man once stated that a disciple should no more conceal his righteousness or his message of salvation than a glowing city should douse its light at night.

When Jesus presented the light metaphor in His Sermon on the Mount, His audience knew exactly what He was talking about. But I wonder if they made the spiritual connection and their responsibility to shine before those around them. And now I ask, "Do we?"

Jesus used light to stress the importance it has to a world that is corrupted by sin and spiritual darkness. Jesus said, *This is who you are—light.* When you know who you are, you will know what to do. We are to burn so we can shine. We are to give light to all, and that means everyone we meet.

📖 What did Jesus command us to do as light?

_____

When Jesus said, "You are the light of the world," He was alluding to the words of Isaiah:

> Nevertheless the gloom will not be upon her who is distressed, as when at first He lightly esteemed the land of Zebulun and the land of Naphtali, and afterward more heavily oppressed her, by the way of the sea, beyond the Jordan, in Galilee of the Gentiles. The people who walked in darkness have seen a great light; those who dwelt in the land of the shadow of death, upon them a light has shined (Isaiah 9:1–2).

> I, the Lord, have called You in righteousness, and will hold Your hand; I will keep You and give You as a covenant to the people, as a light to the Gentiles (Isaiah 42:6).

> Indeed He says, "It is too small a thing that You should be My Servant to raise up the tribes of Jacob, and to restore the preserved ones of Israel; I will also give You as a light to the Gentiles, that You should be My salvation to the ends of the earth" (Isaiah 49:6).

📖 How do the verses in Isaiah 9:1–2; 42:6; and 49:6 relate to what Jesus shared with those on the mountainside about the importance of light?

💜 Keep Me Burning

When Jesus tells you that you are light, He wants you to understand that the light is for "all," that is, the whole world. As a Christian, you are a part of His ministry on the earth, and you are to share the gospel daily with those you contact.

In keeping with the above quotation from Isaiah, the present world is in distress, and people do walk in darkness. As people who are light, we have a great responsibility to share that light with others. You have seen the Great Light. He lives within you. You know the way of salvation, and it is through Jesus Christ. Jesus wants you to make sure as "light in the darkness" that you are ready to share what you know with everyone. "Light is not our good deeds but the means by which people can see that they are good."[14]

He who follows Me shall not walk in darkness.

I love the way *Eerdmans' Handbook to the Bible* puts it: "Here and now these are the ones who put the seasoning into life, who stop the rot, who light up the way. By what they do and say and how they react, they show men something of what God himself is like."[15]

Note the following passages:

- "All authority has been given to Me in heaven and on earth. Go therefore and make disciples of all the nations, baptizing them in the name of the Father and of the Son and of the Holy Spirit, teaching them to observe all things that I have commanded you; and lo, I am with you always, even to the end of the age" (Matthew 28:18–20).

- "Then the master said to the servant, 'Go out into the highways and hedges, and compel them to come in, that my house may be filled'" (Luke 14:23).

- "Whatever I tell you in the dark, speak in the light; and what you hear in the ear, preach on the housetops" (Matthew 10:27).

- "I am the light of the world. He who follows Me shall not walk in darkness, but have the light of life" (John 8:12).

- "For we do not preach ourselves, but Christ Jesus the Lord, and ourselves your servants for Jesus' sake. For it is the God who commanded light to shine out of darkness who has shone in our hearts to give the light of the knowledge of the glory of God in the face of Jesus Christ" (2 Corinthians 4:5–6).

These verses are a portrait of discipleship. Since we have been united with Christ, we share a spiritual union with Him. He gives us a charge to reveal His light to those around us. It is not of our own doing, but it is through Him who lives in us. The world around us should see the radiant light of the Lord within us.

As true disciples, how are we to be an extension of Jesus' ministry today?

_____

In what place on earth does Jesus forbid us to go and share His message? (See Matthew 28:19–20; Luke 14:23.)

_____

Why would Jesus want us to proclaim the good news from the rooftops (Matthew 10:27)?

_____

📖 What charge are we given in 2 Corinthians 4:5–6?

_____

❤️ Light Your Lamp and Let It Shine

Because of the narrow entrance into the harbor, a signalman was always stationed to bring large vessels safely to their moorings. One stormy night, a ship crashed because the captain could not see the signals. The signalman was summoned to court.

The judge asked, "Were you on duty the night of the accident?"

"Yes, I was."

"Did you have your lamps with you?"

"Yes, I did." He showed the lamps to the courtroom.

"Did you properly wave the lamps to warn the captain?"

"Yes."

After a few more questions, the judge dismissed the case. The signalman later told a friend, "I am glad the judge did not ask me if my lamps were lighted. I forgot to do that." A ship had crashed into the rocky shore on that dark night because a signalman had meticulously followed all his orders—except one.

📖 What will prevent you from becoming a signalman that has forgotten to turn on your light?

_____

📖 Those who do not know the Lord are as a ship sailing in the dark. How does this story help you to sympathize more with those around you who don't know Christ?

_____

📖 Do you believe their existence is a scary one? How so?

_____

By using the light metaphor, Jesus is reinforcing the importance of our mission. Just as He said you are salt, He says you are light. Jesus doesn't present that to us for thought, discussion, or debate. He states it for another reason. Jesus tells us we are the light of the world because He is the light who dwells in us.

I am the light of the world. He who follows Me shall not walk in darkness, but have the light of life (John 8:12).

 Shine His Light

Jesus is the Light that illuminates our way to a fuller experience with God. He is the way for those who live in darkness to come to the light. I want a fuller experience with God, and one of the ways to enhance my relationship with Him is to allow His light to shine through me. When His light shines through me, others will see it. Look around you; people everywhere are hurting from the brokenness of this sin-cursed world. Their lives are falling to pieces. As followers of Christ, we have the answer. Jesus is the healing salve that can put broken hearts back together with His peace. Light bearers want to share His peace with others.

■■ What is the only way broken lives are put back together?

_____

■■ Find the song "Bring Christ Your Broken Life" and read the words aloud. What does it mean to be marred by sin? How can you bring Him your every care—great or small? Do you need to bring Christ your weariness?

_____

📖 Contrast those who bring light upon entering a room with those who bring gloom. Why do Christians need to be mindful of their countenances?

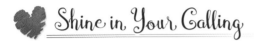

Shine in Your Calling

For he who has died has been freed from sin. Now if we died with Christ, we believe that we shall also live with Him, knowing that Christ, having been raised from the dead, dies no more. Death no longer has dominion over Him. For the death that He died, He died to sin once for all; but the life that He lives, He lives to God. Likewise you also, reckon yourselves to be dead indeed to sin, but alive to God in Christ Jesus our Lord (Romans 6:7–11).

When Jesus lives in us and we yield to His teachings, we come to understand that our influence is vitally important. Those who don't know Christ will see the light He brings to our lives.

They may see your good works and glorify your Father in heaven.

His light in us points the way. His light in us brings illumination to a dark path. It is by our example that others can see His light, and we must not allow sin to "cover our shine." Because He lives in us, we should sin less and less. What we do and say make a difference. Our conduct and speech determine how brightly we shine.

In a *Peanuts* cartoon, Peppermint Patty addressed Charlie Brown: "Guess what, Chuck. The first day of school I got sent to the principal's office. It was your fault, Chuck."

Charlie Brown responded: "My fault? How could it be my fault? Why do you say everything is my fault?"

"You're my friend, aren't you, Chuck? You should have been a better influence on me."

Peppermint Patty was trying to pass the buck, but as a Christian, being light is your calling, and you must not forget it. You are called to influence those in darkness because you have been transformed by Christ who dwells in you. Because of this, you have a responsibility to other Christians and to the world.

📖 What does Ephesians 5:6–14 teach us about our example?

_____

📖 What are some "deeds of darkness" that your light might expose?

_____

📖 What is the fruit of light (Ephesians 5:8–10)?

_____

📖 How are you trying to learn what is pleasing to the Lord (v. 10)?

_____

📖 How will this help your light to shine brighter?

_____

 ## You Are Salt and Light

As you follow Jesus, His light guides your daily walk. Christians, and even the world, can see a huge difference in those who follow Jesus and those who do not. Any time light dispels darkness, things should get better. Right?

Paul tells us, "Do not grow weary in doing good" (2 Thessalonians 3:13). So why not make a difference in this world? Jesus says we can. You are salt; you are light. That's who you are.

So strike a match or flip the switch. Set a fire deep in your soul that will shine His light in this dark world, and don't forget who you are. You are light; shine brightly.

> Become blameless and harmless . . . in the midst of a crooked and perverse generation, among whom you shine as lights in the world, holding fast the word of life, so that I may rejoice in the day of Christ that I have not run in vain or labored in vain (Philippians 2:15–16).

We are called to spread the news,
To tell the world the simple truth;
Jesus came to save, there's freedom in His Name,
So let His love break through.

We are the light of the world,
We are the city on a hill;
We are the light of the world,
We gotta, we gotta, we gotta let the light shine.

—excerpt from "We Are" by Kari Jobe

7

SHACKLES
and Chains

MARK 5:1–20

Tell them what great things the Lord has done for you, and how He has had compassion on you.

—Mark 5:19

A co-worker asked a recent convert, "What is it like to be a Christian?" She replied, "It's like being a pumpkin in a field. Jesus picks you up from the patch, brings you in, and washes all the dirt off. Then He cuts the top off and scoops out all the yucky stuff. He removes the seeds of doubt, hate, greed, fear, shamefulness, uncertainty, and so much more. Then He carves you a new face and puts a light inside you that shines for all the world to see."

As childlike as this story may sound, that's what happens when you meet Jesus and allow Him to do what only He can do for you.

Unshackled

When you allow Jesus to remove all the weights that you hold onto, or maybe the weights that hold onto you, transformation comes. Peace overwhelms you. That's what it is like when you meet Jesus. And in a world full of chaos and confusion, isn't peace exactly what you need?

What does *peace* mean? What does it look like? Jesus said, "Peace I leave with you, My peace I give to you" (John 14:27).

> Greek definition: "Peace" is from the word *eirēnē*, which means "a state of untroubled, undisturbed well-being."

Now for clarity's sake, let's insert the meaning of *peace* in John 14:27:

A state of untroubled, undisturbed well-being I leave with you, My untroubled, undisturbed well-being I give to you.

As we encounter turmoil, brokenness, chaos, and emptiness almost on a daily basis, we must understand that Jesus left us His peace. He came, He lived, and He died so that we might experience untroubled, undisturbed well-being, even in the middle of chaos.

Man of the Tombs

One particular event in Mark's account of the Gospel grips my heart. Every time I begin to read about the "man of the tombs"—the Gadarene demonic—my heart breaks for him. Think of the kind of life he endured; he truly lived among the dead. But here's the good news that causes my heart to rejoice. When he met Jesus, everything changed.

Have you ever encountered someone who has struggled to make real sense of life? Have you ever wondered how someone could end up living in a dysfunctional, broken lifestyle? Perhaps you've watched as they kept repeating the same patterns of behavior that had them bound and shackled. I have witnessed individuals who struggle with a life of regret and shame. Those situations are difficult to watch. I have seen firsthand what happens to those who cannot forgive themselves for personal mistakes. Not only can they not forgive themselves, but they also cannot forgive others. Have you watched as friends or family have made their own prisons, not of bars and locked doors, but emotional prisons of self-hatred and shame? I call that type of life "emotional and mental lock down."

Many people become the way they are because of unusual circumstances, bad choices, or evil influences. I no longer believe that people just "become" who they are overnight. Maybe their lives can be better explained by understanding that many are bound in emotional graveyards by their own regret and shame. They exist as the "living dead." That is exactly how the Gadarene man of the tombs lived.

> Then they came to the other side of the sea, to the country of the Gadarenes. And when [Jesus] had come out of the boat, immediately there met Him out of the tombs a man with an unclean spirit, who had his dwelling among the tombs; and no one could bind him, not even with chains, because he had often been bound with shackles and chains. And the chains had been pulled apart by him, and the shackles broken in pieces; neither could anyone tame him. And always, night and day, he was in the mountains and in the tombs, crying out and cutting himself with stones (Mark 5:1–5).

Come to Me, all you who labor and are heavy laden, and I will give you rest.

In verses 3–5 of this text we see:

- He lives among the dead.

- He is out of control.

- He is in torment.

- He is harming himself.

The man of the tombs lived away from other people, alone, and worst of all, he lived in a graveyard among the dead. Inside he raged and warred against himself. That poor demon-possessed man had superhuman strength. He was able to break the chains and shackles that others had placed on him. He must have been such a threat to those living in the city that the citizens decided to shackle and chain him to keep him away from them. But nothing they did kept him at bay.

Lonnie Jones, a Christian speaker and counselor, gives two possible reasons this man was shackled:

- People said, "We've got to do something *with* this man!"
- People said, "We've got to do something *for* this man. He is hurting himself and others."

The solution for both groups was "shackles and chains," but those were not what he needed. He needed Jesus.

📖 How is it possible to believe we are helping others, when in reality we are only causing them more pain?

📖 What are some of the "shackles and chains" others have placed on you?

📖 Why should you be quick to offer Jesus to people before you offer them anything else? Why don't you?

❤️ Calm for the Inside Storm

When he saw Jesus from afar, he ran and worshiped Him. And he cried out with a loud voice and said, "What have I to do with You, Jesus, Son of the Most High God? I implore You by God that You do not torment me." For He said to him, "Come out of the man,

74

unclean spirit!" Then He asked him, "What is your name?" And he answered, saying, "My name is Legion; for we are many." Also, he begged Him earnestly that He would not send them out of the country (Mark 5:6–10).

Even though the Bible does not say, it is almost obvious that Jesus came to the country of the Gadarenes to meet this man. Jesus had specifically said to His disciples, "Let us cross over to the other side" (Mark 4:35). Then in the midst of the Sea of Galilee, a great storm arose. On that occasion, Jesus said His most beloved words: "Peace be still. . . . Why are you so fearful? How is it that you have no faith?" (Mark 4:39–40).

Do not fear . . . you are of more value than many sparrows.

Most of us are familiar with the account of Jesus' calming a storm outside the boat, but the greater lesson is that He calmed a storm inside the boat, the one raging inside His frightened disciples. What does that teach us? That He can calm a raging storm inside you and me.

Place of Tombs and Pigs

The entire region of Decapolis was pagan, a place of pagan cult worship, populated with Gentiles, detestable to a Jewish man. What's more, their favored animal was the pig. The Gadarene region was known as the land of the pigs; pigs for sale for sacrifices. Can you imagine the faces of Jesus' disciples as they boarded the ship and headed across the sea to such a place? Why would anyone of Jewish descent want to go to Gadarene? They didn't want to be near pigs; they didn't want to be near anyone who had anything to do with pigs. Also, if they had known their trip would lead them to a cemetery, they would have been even more alarmed. Touching a dead body rendered one ceremonially unclean (Numbers 9:6–7). Just to be near a cemetery would have made them uncomfortable.

📖 Before Jesus came, what might have been a typical day for the demon-possessed man?

_____

📖 How can you be alive physically but exist as the "living dead"?

_____

📖 Jesus' interaction with the man of the tombs demonstrates the uniqueness of Jesus and further defines His earthly mission. What are your thoughts about Jesus' going to the Gadarenes? How does this help you to understand the nature of Jesus?

_____

How Much the Lord Has Done for You

Now a large herd of swine was feeding there near the mountains. And all the demons begged Him, saying, "Send us to the swine, that we may enter them." And at once Jesus gave them permission. Then the unclean spirits went out and entered the swine (there were about two thousand); and the herd ran violently down the steep place into the sea, and drowned in the sea. Now those who fed the swine fled, and they told it in the city and in the country. And they went out to see what it was that had happened. Then they came to Jesus, and saw the one who had been demon-possessed and had the legion, sitting and clothed and in his right mind. And they were afraid. And those who saw it told them how it happened to him who had been demon-possessed, and about the swine. Then they began to plead with Him to depart from their region. And when He got into the boat, he who had been demon-possessed begged Him that he might be with Him. However, Jesus did not permit him, but said to him, "Go home to your friends, and tell

76

them what great things the Lord has done for you, and how He has had compassion on you." And he departed and began to proclaim in Decapolis all that Jesus had done for him; and all marveled (Mark 5:11–20).

📖 What does Jesus' interaction with the demonic man teach us regarding His feelings about all people?

_____

📖 How can you tell others about Jesus and what He can do for them?

_____

📖 List three ways Jesus has changed you.

_____

📖 What are the red-letter words of Jesus after He cast the demons out of the man of the tombs and set him free? (See verse 19.)

_____

The demon-free man begged Jesus to stay with him and be with him. I can only imagine how he felt after he was "free at last." The joy and calm he must have experienced for the first time in years had to be overwhelming. Jesus rarely told those He healed to go and tell others what He had done, but He did on this occasion: "Go home to your friends, and tell them what great things the Lord has done for you, and how He has had compassion on you."

Can you imagine what the people of that city thought as they witnessed the great transformation of this man? I can hear the whispers and see the stares as he walks about town and tells everyone about his encounter with Jesus. I know for sure that if this had happened in my hometown, the local restaurants would be filled with people talking about the man down the road who was now unshackled and unchained. The news was billboard worthy: *Local Man*

Set Free! Maybe there would have been a "before" and "after" picture celebrating his transformation.

📖 How did Jesus help the demonic man to become light to a dark and dying world?

_____

📖 Imagine the story the demonic man told about how Jesus set him free. What impact do you suppose his message had in this region?

_____

📖 How can you use your past to tell others how Jesus has set you free?

_____

Have you forgotten that Jesus is the one who has the power to change lives? The man of the tombs stands as an awesome reminder of our Lord's transforming ability. Once you meet Jesus, you are never the same again. When He says to those who know Him, "Go in peace" (Mark 5:34; Luke 7:50; 8:48), you can believe that He has the power to set you free. "Therefore if the Son makes you free, you shall be free indeed" (John 8:36).

Bob Bennett writes a beautiful description of the man of the tombs. His story is portrayed in true poetic form from the moments before he meets Jesus until Jesus sets him free. Each time I read the poem, I feel as though I am watching the demoniac's life unfold before my eyes. At the climax of the poem, I find myself smiling and feeling exhilarated to know the unforgettable effect of an encounter with Jesus on one life.

Arise, take up your bed, and go to your house.

MAN OF THE TOMBS

Man of the tombs—
He lives in a place where no one goes,
And he tears at himself,
And lives with a pain that no one knows.
He counts himself dead among the living;
He knows no mercy and no forgiving.
Deep in the night he's driven to cry out loud.
Can you hear him cry out loud?

Man of the tombs—
Possessed by an unseen enemy,
He breaks every chain
And mistakes his freedom for being free.
Shame and shamelessness equally there,
Like a random toss of a coin in the air.
Man of the tombs—he's driven to cry out loud.

"Underneath this thing that I've become,
A fading memory of flesh and blood,
I curse the womb, I bless the grave.
I've lost my heart; I cannot be saved.
Like those who fear me, I'm afraid.
Like those I've hurt, I can feel pain.
Naked now before my sin,
And these stones that cut against my skin,
Some try to touch me, but no one can,
For man of the tombs I am."

Down at the shoreline
Two sets of footprints meet.
One voice is screaming,
The other voice begins to speak.
In only a moment and only a word

The evil departs like a thundering herd.
Man of the tombs—He hears this cry out loud.

"Underneath this thing that you've become
I see a man of flesh and blood.
I give you life beyond the grave.
I heal your heart; I come to save.
No need to fear, be not afraid,
This Man of sorrows knows your pain.
I come to take away your sin
And bear its marks upon My skin.
When no one can touch you, still I can,
For Son of God I am."

Dressed now and seated,
Clean in spirit, and healthy of mind,
Man of the tombs,
He begs to follow, but must stay behind.
He'll return to his family with stories to tell
Of mercy and madness, of heaven and hell.
Man of the tombs—soon he will cry out loud.

"Underneath this thing that I once was,
Now I'm a man of flesh and blood.
I have a life beyond the grave.
I found my heart; I can now be saved.
No need to fear; I am not afraid.
This Man of sorrows took my pain.
He comes to take away our sin
And bear its marks upon His skin.
I'm telling you this story because
Man of the tombs I was."

—Bob Bennett[16]

Are you smiling? I thought so.

8

TRANSFORMATION,
Contrast and Application:
Man of the Tombs

Transformation means to change. Every time I see a butterfly, I am reminded of all the changes it went through to become so beautiful. Butterflies are God's way of showing us that when Jesus transforms us into a new creation, someday we will get our wings and fly safely into His arms.

—Debbie Dupuy

This chapter is written differently from the others in this book. As we study the account of the man of the tombs from a historical and cultural background, we will consider other texts to understand further who Jesus is and what He did for those He encountered. The focus of this chapter is transformation. Let's uncover some personal applications from the man of the tombs.

♥ Jesus Knows No Boundaries

Jesus does not limit Himself to regions, cultures, or religious practices that made Jews feel comfortable. He does not recognize caste systems, nor does He promote a "wrong side of the tracks" mentality.

Some people even in the church might turn up their noses or refuse to associate with individuals different from them. Jesus never did that. Everyone has worth and value in His eyes. Jesus loved people—all people. He crossed into territory that was forbidden in the culture of His day when He approached someone considered "unapproachable."

> He left Judea and departed again to Galilee. But He needed to go through Samaria. So He came to a city . . . called Sychar. . . . Now Jacob's well was there. Jesus therefore, being wearied from His journey, sat thus by the well. . . . A woman of Samaria came to draw water. Jesus said to her, "Give Me a drink." . . . Then the woman of Samaria said to Him, "How is it that You, being a Jew, ask a drink from me, a Samaritan woman?" For Jews have no dealings with Samaritans. Jesus answered and said to her, "If you knew the gift of God, and who it is who says to you, 'Give Me a drink,' you would have asked Him, and He would have given you living water. . . . Whoever drinks of this water will thirst again, but whoever drinks of the water that I shall give him will never thirst. But the water that I shall give him will become in him a fountain of water springing up into everlasting life."
>
> The woman said to Him, "Sir, give me this water, that I may not thirst, nor come here to draw." Jesus said to her, "Go, call your husband, and come here." The woman answered and said, "I have no husband." Jesus said to her, "You have well said, 'I have no husband,' for you have had five husbands, and the one whom you now have is not your husband; in that you spoke truly." The woman said to Him, "Sir, I perceive that You are a prophet. Our fathers worshiped on this mountain, and you Jews say that in Jerusalem is the place where one ought to worship." Jesus said to her, "Woman, believe Me, the hour is coming when you will neither on this mountain, nor in Jerusalem, worship the Father. You worship what you do not know; we know what we worship, for salvation is of the Jews. But the hour is coming, and now is, when the true worshipers will worship the Father in spirit and truth; for the Father is seeking such to worship Him. God is Spirit, and those who worship Him must

worship in spirit and truth." The woman said to Him, "I know that Messiah is coming" (who is called Christ). "When He comes, He will tell us all things." Jesus said to her, "I who speak to you am He." . . . The woman then left her waterpot, went her way into the city, and said to the men, "Come, see a Man who told me all things that I ever did. Could this be the Christ?" Then they went out of the city and came to Him (John 4:3–30).

Could This Be the Christ?

The Samaritan woman was astonished by Jesus' asking her for a drink of water. When Jesus lived, there were dividing lines among people. Jewish men did not speak to Samaritans, certainly not to Samaritan women. And it would have been a social no-no for a Jew to drink from a Samaritan vessel, for Jews had no dealings with Samaritans. They were of a mixed race, Jew and Gentile. Racism was alive and well in the first century.

> Jews did not associate with Samaritans: This antagonism goes back to the late sixth and fifth centuries BC when exiled Jews returned to Judah from Babylon, who regarded this mixed populace as unclean. . . . In rabbinical literature, specific prohibitions exclude virtually all contact between the two parties.[17]

Notice Jesus' response to the woman's surprise at His taking notice of her: "If you knew the gift of God, and who it is that says to you, 'Give Me a drink,' you would have asked Him and He would have given you living water" (John 4:10).

What do you learn about Jesus in John 4:3–30 as you relate it to Mark's account of the man of the tombs?

📖 What does Jesus teach us about the value of every person, whether male or female or of a different nationality?

📖 What does Jesus teach us about racism in this passage? Should we label people or use a "caste system" of worthiness?

My husband has worked with people with disabilities for over twenty years. He has witnessed firsthand how others treat them because they are different. It is heartbreaking to watch when people overlook them while speaking to others in the room. It is shameful when health-care workers refuse them the kind of treatment they give to anyone else, and it's disturbing when some people mock and belittle them because of their disabilities.

What I know for sure is that if Jesus walked into a room with a special-needs individual, He would be the first to acknowledge that person. I can picture Jesus sitting and talking with that person, just as He would anyone else. Jesus came to teach us that all people have worth and value in His eyes. With Jesus there is no race barrier, culture barrier, or socioeconomic barrier. He loves you if you are heavy, thin, black, white, rich, poor, kind, or unkind. He loves you in spite of your past actions or background.

📖 Is there a person, from those on skid row to those who are regarded as elite and powerful, whom Jesus doesn't care about? Support your answer.

📖 How did Jesus treat the non-Jewish woman who had had five husbands?

📖 What do His actions say about His love for you?

💙 Jesus Is Accepted or Rejected

Back to the man of the tombs. The demoniac ran to meet Jesus: "When he saw Jesus from afar, he ran and worshiped Him" (Mark 5:6). The townsfolk ran away: "So those who fed the swine fled, and they told it in the city and in the country. And they went out to see what it was that had happened" (Mark 5:14). At the end of the account, the townspeople began to beg Him to "depart from their region." However, the man of the tombs "begged Him that he might be with Him."

There are many speculations as to why the townspeople asked Jesus to leave. One consideration is that He caused them to lose their income. But they might have asked Him to leave because of fear, because people tend to fear what they do not understand. Whatever the reason, we must understand that not everyone is willing to accept Jesus, nor do they wish to follow Him. But it is clear: we either accept Him or we reject Him.

But Jesus was no stranger to rejection. Even in His hometown as He began His ministry, Jesus' presence was met with both admiration and hostility:

> So all bore witness to Him, and marveled at the gracious words which proceeded out of His mouth. And they said, "Is this not Joseph's son?" He said to them, "You will surely say this proverb to Me, 'Physician, heal yourself! Whatever we have heard done in Capernaum, do also here in Your country.'" Then He said, "Assuredly, I say to you, no prophet is accepted in his own country. But I tell you truly, many widows were in Israel in the days of Elijah, when the heaven was shut up three years and six months, and there was a great famine throughout all the land; but to none of them was Elijah sent except to Zarephath, in the region of Sidon,

to a woman who was a widow. And many lepers were in Israel in the time of Elisha the prophet, and none of them was cleansed except Naaman the Syrian." So all those in the synagogue, when they heard these things, were filled with wrath, and rose up and thrust Him out of the city; and they led Him to the brow of the hill on which their city was built, that they might throw Him down over the cliff. Then passing through the midst of them, He went His way (Luke 4:22–30).

📖 Notice the red-letter words of Jesus. Why does He remind them of Elijah and Elisha?

_____

📖 What indicates that He called their attention to the fact that God's people had rejected Him long ago?

_____

📖 How is it possible that "religious people" can end up rejecting Jesus?

_____

📖 How do we know that Jesus did not stop teaching after this rejection?

_____

📖 What can we learn from Jesus' example?

_____

Many Reject Jesus Today

Have you ever witnessed a rejection of Jesus? I will never forget a Bible study a friend and I were conducting with a young man who had been attending worship. As we began to study baptism with him, he said, "I refuse to accept what you are telling me." My friend said to him, "Dear one, you aren't rejecting us, you are rejecting the words of the Bible and the Lord." But he refused to accept the truth of God's Word and it discouraged us. He left that night, and we began to pray for him. Two days later he called from work and asked my husband to baptize him, which he did that very afternoon. Sometimes, it just takes a little time for people to meditate on a new biblical principle, especially if it is contrary to what they have believed for a long time.

📖 When people reject the gospel, why might it discourage you? How do you prevent discouragement?

_____

📖 Should we take discouragement personally? What must we remember when people reject the gospel?

_____

💜 Jesus Has All Authority

We notice in our text that the word *beg* or *begging* is used repeatedly. Read different versions for other translations, and remember these points about Mark 5:10, 12, 17, and 18:

- The possessed man begged Jesus.
- The demons begged Jesus.
- The people begged Jesus.
- The demoniac once again begged Jesus.

There was a whole lot of begging going on that day in the Gadarenes. The fascinating point of all of this begging is that Jesus was the authority. He had the authority to cast out demons who recognized Him as Jesus, the Son of the Most High God. The demons also recognized His authority by asking Him to send them into the pigs. Jesus granted that permission, and in so doing, reinforced His authority.

Luke records another example of Jesus' authority over a demon:

> Now in the synagogue there was a man who had a spirit of an unclean demon. And he cried out with a loud voice, saying, "Let us alone! What have we to do with You, Jesus of Nazareth? Did You come to destroy us? I know who You are—the Holy One of God!" But Jesus rebuked him, saying, "Be quiet, and come out of him!" And when the demon had thrown him in their midst, it came out of him and did not hurt him. Then they were all amazed and spoke among themselves, saying, "What a word this is! For with authority and power He commands the unclean spirits, and they come out" (Luke 4:33–36).

📖 What do you notice about Jesus' words in Luke 4:35? How do they reveal His authority?

_____

📖 Notice also what the people said about the words of Jesus. What are the key words (Luke 4:36)?

_____

💜 Jesus Transforms from the Inside Out

Before Jesus entered the land of the Gadarenes, the man of the tombs lived in a pitiful condition. He cried out day and night, he was naked, and he cut himself. He lived among the dead. He demonstrated amazing strength as he broke his shackles and chains continually. After meeting Jesus, what happened?

- He regained his right mind.
- He immediately dressed himself.

- He stopped harming himself and became a man at peace.
- He went from a tormented life to a life of peace and joy.
- He was transformed!

This is an amazing event of transformation and the mighty power of Jesus. Do you believe that Jesus has all authority to transform your life? Have you forgotten that Jesus has the power to transform the lives of others as well?

A BROKEN ROAD

My dear and wonderful friend was recovering from her addiction to methamphetamine. Her story is much like the man in the tombs. She lived separated from her family, and she, too, was hurting herself by abusing her body with drugs. She was as the living dead and had lived her life on the broken road. She had a life of hardship because of poor choices and bad relationships. She was awaiting trial for making and selling meth, so as a last resort, she decided to try Jesus. We became friends through a Bible study.

When we first became friends, she and I studied two or three times a week. I will never forget our first session. Her speech was slurred, and she was shaking terribly, as any meth victim does when going through withdrawal. The more we studied, the more she seemed to come to life—just like the man of the tombs. My friend became convinced that Jesus had a lot to offer. Once she learned what she needed to do to be in Christ, she put Him on in baptism and had her sins washed away (Acts 2:38; Galatians 3:27).

My sweet friend requested baptism in the dead of winter, and the water heater was broken. We carried pails of hot water from our fellowship building to the baptistery and poured them into the water, hoping to knock off the chill. She went bravely into the water. When she was raised up out of the water, she literally shook like an old wet hound. I will never forget that cold night in January. I will never ever forget how knowing Jesus and His precious Word changed her life.

Now take a deep breath because what I am about to tell you may seem incredible. I served with my new sister in Christ and witnessed her conduct as a new Christian. She went to trial. When the judge granted her probation, he then added, "I don't know why I am doing this but I am going to do this for you." My friend was then asked by a drug rehab group to come and share her story about getting off the meth and how her life had changed. She was glad to do so.

She never went through rehab. She came off the meth with the divine help of Jesus Christ. (I know the statistics that exist about recovery outside of rehab, but I am telling you the truth!) She told everyone she met how much Jesus had done for her, just as the man of the tombs had told about the great things the Lord had done for him.

———————•———————

Unfortunately, no part of my friend's life was a fairy tale, not even her life after conversion. She had been transformed, but the consequences of her former bad choices kept following her. My dear sister in Christ had bouts with drug cravings, which were minute-by-minute challenges with which to cope. (We have an enemy that is alive and well, and his name is Satan.) She developed pancreatic cancer, but even then she told me, "I thank God for this cancer because maybe this is His protection and care for me not to go back to the drugs." It was difficult to see her suffer, but I had to accept His plan. My friend passed away with the full assurance of God's grace and comfort. I fully believe that now she is truly transformed and that she is safe in the arms of Jesus.

▊▊ How does my friend's situation help remind us of what a life surrendered to Jesus can do for others, even a meth addict?

📖 If you know someone with a similar story, be ready to share that information with the class.

Jesus Is Not Always Recognized as God

During the storm, the disciples didn't know who Jesus really was. We know this because of the question they asked in Mark 4:41 after He calmed the storm on the Sea of Galilee: "Who can this be, that even the wind and the sea obey Him?" However, the demons recognized Him and fully believed in Him (Mark 5:7).

📖 Since it is possible to be with Jesus and not recognize who He is, what precautions should we take in our daily walk with Him?

Jesus Wants You to Share What He Has Done for You

The man of the tombs was the first Gentile that Jesus commanded to go and tell others about Him. The region where he returned was Decapolis, meaning "ten cities," although at the time of the miracle, the region had come to include more than ten cities. Decapolis began on the east side of the Sea of Galilee and extended southward some fifty miles. The population was predominately Gentile. The man of the tombs had an opportunity to spread the good news of Jesus to the masses in a place where the disciples who traveled with Jesus did not preach.

James says, "Every good gift and every perfect gift is from above, and comes down from the Father of lights, with whom there is no variation or shadow of turning" (James 1:17). The Father of lights is God, creator of the lights that rule the day and regulate the seasons.

"No variation or shadow of turning" alludes to the fact that God's nature is unchanging and that His promises are secure. Jesus is sure; He is unchanging; there is no variation; He is the creator of all things (John 1:1–3; Colossians 1:15–20).

When Jesus told the man of the tombs, "Go home to your friends, and tell them what great things the Lord has done for you," he obeyed. We have the awesome responsibility to tell others about Jesus—who He is and what He can do for those who obey and trust Him. Can you imagine all of the people who came to know Christ because of this man's testimony?

📖 List four great things the Lord has done for you.

📖 What special situations would you share with someone about one of the great things the Lord has done for you?

TRAIN YOURSELF TO SEE HIS GIFTS

The word *intentional* is used a lot in subjects relating to marriage, parenting, and business. Being intentional in these areas proves effective; however, Christians must be intentional people in all aspects of life. As followers of Jesus, we must recognize the good things the Lord has done for us, as well as the pitfalls that may realistically lead us astray.

How can you share Jesus unless you train yourself to see what is good in your life? Every generous act and every perfect gift comes from God. Intend to see His gifts.

What might keep you from recognizing the "good and perfect" gifts from God? Negativity? Discontentment? Bitterness? Unforgiveness? Do you see why you must become intentional? Being negative only makes a difficult journey more difficult.

You may be given a cactus, but you don't have to sit on it. Don't expect the worst in others or situations. Don't lose hope and let your weaknesses and insecurities limit you. The only place you have a fighting chance is in the Lord's presence, in the light of His Word, and in all of the good things He provides. Be among godly people who are free of negativity, hopelessness, and discontentment, otherwise you will be robbed of recognizing all the good that God is doing.

RECORD WHAT HE DOES FOR YOU

For many years, I have recorded my prayer requests in my journal, as well as the good gifts God has provided. My notes serve as reminders of God's faithfulness. These recorded blessings also help me to focus my mind on what I might otherwise miss had I not written them down.

Years ago, my good friend Lawanda encouraged me to develop the journaling habit. One evening as I was cleaning out an upstairs storage room, I ran across one of my old prayer journals. I began to read the requests and remember the worries and frustrations with which I was dealing at the time. As I read, the tears began to flow. My heart was full because I had seen the mighty and magnificent way the Lord had taken care of me and my family. The wonderful thing about my requests to God was that He fulfilled them more completely than I had asked Him.

I called my husband. "What's wrong?" he asked. "You've been crying. Is everything okay?" I read him the prayer journal that evening. He was so moved by God's faithfulness that he, too, began to cry. Too often we forget to stop and think of all the wonderful things the Lord does and provides for us. When we recall His faithfulness, our faith in Him is strengthened.

Several years ago I challenged myself to a write down one thousand good gifts from God. Every day I recorded all of the good things the Lord had provided. That helped me to become intentional and to focus on God's continual provisions. I surpassed my goals, and that habit remains an ongoing challenge to this day. I challenge you to write down the gifts God provides you each day. In so doing, you will transform your thoughts and develop a renewed perspective on life.

📖 How will writing down your prayers help you?

_____

📖 How will making a written record of God's work in your life help you to see more clearly the good gifts He provides each day?

_____

Jesus Is Stronger Than Your Mightiest Demon

The name Legion (Mark 5:9) indicates the strength of the demons. A Roman military legion consisted of about six thousand soldiers. Mark reveals that two thousand pigs rushed down a steep bank into the sea when the demons entered them. His many demons explain the townspeople's inability to restrain him. His supernatural strength was so great that nothing could hold him.

The application for us is that nothing is too powerful for Jesus in our lives. Nothing! Jesus is more powerful than any "demon" you face. You may be tormented, bound, and feel as if you are living among the dead. But when you allow Jesus to take control of your life, the chains break and freedom comes.

📖 What "demons" are you facing?

_____

📖 What powerful thing controls, or attempts to control, your life?

_____

📖 What "demons" do you need the Son to expel from you?

Do you have problems with anger and bitterness or hatred and jealousy? Do you have too much pride? Do you feel inferior to those around you? Ask Him to set you free; He will.

When you feel tormented by the demons of life, get into the Word. Find scriptures that relate to your problems and write them down. Use them to help you overcome what is tormenting you. Memorize, quote, and post them in areas where you need the encouragement.

RECOGNIZE SATAN'S SLOP

The pigs in this account demonstrate their senseless and destructive nature, just like Satan and his tactics. Pigs like slop and Satan offers you slop as well. This is a perfect picture of Satan's ultimate aim for the world. He is our adversary; he lives to oppose the child of God. Satan wants you to give up and become discouraged in the faith. He is betting that he can make you quit.

📖 When Satan was described as a thief, Jesus warned that he comes for what purpose (John 10:10)?

📖 What is Peter's warning about Satan (1 Peter 5:8)?

📖 Describe Satan's character (John 8:44).

Satan is a liar. His aim is to make you believe the lies he tells you about yourself. For example, Satan tempts you so that you say, "Nobody loves me; nobody cares about me; I am not good enough; no one accepts me." Those are a few of his lies among many others. He lies to you about who you are. If you believe him, you will become discouraged.

📖 Why must you be careful with your "thought life" (Colossians 2:8)?

_____

📖 How can Satan use the philosophy of this world and human tradition to influence us?

_____

FIGHT SATAN'S "SLOP DARTS"

Paul's words in Ephesians 6:16 explain Satan's tactics: "Above all, taking the shield of faith with which you will be able to quench all the fiery darts of the wicked one." Satan hurls "slop darts" our way, and we must be on guard as 1 Peter 5:8 explains.

So you've never heard of a slop dart. Don't go looking for it in Webster's dictionary. The reason? "Slop dart" isn't there. It's a term I invented. So here is my definition: _Anything that is hurled at us by Satan that can take our focus away from God and His power._ Slop darts keep us from living a life of freedom and joy. Like my friend who had been addicted to meth, slop darts were difficult for her to resist. Her life fell apart because of slop darts.

By the way, you don't have to be an addict to be overcome by Satan's slop darts. We can be overtaken in the constant battle of our minds and in our attitudes. However, if we are on guard and realize the enemy's tactics, we can overcome anything he shoots our way.

📖 What can we do to be ready for battle (Ephesians 6:14–17)?

_____

📖 Paul describes several pieces of defensive armor, but what offensive weapon are we to use in battle?

_____

BEWARE OF THE CULTURAL DEMON

Pigs are a great metaphor for the culture in America. Pigs wallow in mud. Run one through a car wash, if you like, and he will instinctively go back to the mud hole. They eat slop, and they are not concerned about the ingredients. In fact, wallowing in the mud and eating slop is part of their nature. I have to ask, "Has our culture been overtaken by slop darts?"

In a 2014 Barna Research study, more Americans identified themselves as "non-churched" than at any time in the history of this nation.[18] We are now living in a post-Christian era in the United States. The breakdown of the home, the influence of secularism in public schools (no mention of God, prayer, or moral training), and the removal of anything biblical from society have had a tremendous effect on the culture. People have turned to secularism as their guide for living. We are in a "live and let live" society.

While we, as God's people, may not be eating slop or wallowing in the mud, we must consider how our culture may be influencing us. We may be filling our minds with slop by allowing the news, TV programs, music, and ungodly Internet sites to shape our thinking. We could be wallowing in negativity, discontentment, and bitterness. We must understand that what we feed on has a spiritual connection to us. As children of God, we have one source to filter everything we hear, see, and believe to be true. That source is our standard—the Word of God. If we allow our minds to be shaped by the standards in our culture, we are living like pigs, and if we are not careful, we will eventually end up in the devil's slaughter house.

▌▌ What do you identify as Satan's biggest slop dart in our culture?

Jesus Will Never Leave You the Way He Finds You

The goal for this chapter was to contrast the man of the tombs before and after his transformation and make practical application. Jesus did not leave the man full of demons. Anyone who truly wants to know Jesus and follow Him, quickly understands that He will never leave you the way He found you. With Jesus you can experience a 180-degree turn, just like the man of the tombs. However, like the transformed man, you must realize that some will be afraid of your transformation. Sometimes people will leave you because you have been changed.

A few of the lines from the song "In Christ Alone" describe a heart transformed by Jesus, even when people leave us:

> Sin's curse has lost its grip on me;
> For I am His and He is mine,
> Bought with the precious blood of Christ.
>
> —Stuart Richard Townsend

■■ Have you ever known someone who lost friends after becoming a Christian? How would you advise such a person?

_____

■■ Why do family members sometimes reject one of their own because that person decided to follow Christ?

_____

■■ Research the song "In Christ Alone" and sing or read all the verses. Find a scripture to support the statement, "No power of hell, no scheme of man, can ever pluck me from His hand."

_____

♥ Jesus Practiced the Law of Love

In Mark 1:40–45 when Jesus healed the leper, He strictly warned him, "See that you say nothing to anyone; but go your way, show yourself to the priest, and offer for your cleansing those things which Moses commanded, as a testimony to them" (v. 44). Yet He told the man of the tombs: "Go home to your friends, and tell them what great things the Lord has done for you" (Mark 5:19).

Jesus often told those whom He healed not to tell others. Maybe that was because Jesus did not want people to come to Him merely for physical benefits. But Jesus wanted the leper to go to the priest to comply with the regulations of Leviticus 14, as a testimony to them, so that they would know that Jesus did not disregard ceremonial law. However, touching a leper was forbidden under Jewish law, but Jesus overruled the ceremonial law by the law of love. He touched the leper because He loved him.

- When Jesus healed the blind man, "He sent him away to his house, saying, "Neither go into the town, nor tell anyone in the town" (Mark 8:26).

- Jesus asked the disciples, "Who do you say that I am?" When they answered Him, He strictly warned them to tell no one (Mark 8:27–30). He warned others in a similar way. (See Matthew 9:30; 12:16; 16:20; Mark 1:44; Luke 5:14.)

The events of Jesus' ministry were often in conflict with Jewish politics.

- *Jealousy and Hatred of the Religious Leaders.* Jesus often moved away from situations in which Jewish leaders might be overly aroused and have easy access in apprehending Him (Luke 20:20). Jesus had to manage His execution—the time and place.

- *Crowd Control* (Matthew 8:18). As more and more individuals flocked to Jesus, the crowds became too large to handle effectively. Jesus moved to less demanding crowds in less prominent areas.

- *False Expectations.* Less obvious but quite clear in Jewish history is that the Zealots were looking for a Messiah to lead them in a revolt against the Romans.[19]

- *Timing.* Jesus often told those He healed not to say anything because He knew the time for His sacrificial death had not yet come. He had a mission to fulfill. He knew that the crowds would invoke more hostility toward Him among the Jewish leaders, and He wanted to make sure, at the time of His death, that He had fulfilled all the Father had given Him to do.

 ## What Did You Learn?

- Jesus knows no geographical boundaries.
- Jesus is accepted or rejected.
- Jesus has all authority.
- Jesus transforms from inside out.
- Jesus is not always recognized as God.
- Jesus wants you to share what He has done for you.
- Jesus is stronger than your mightiest demon.
- Jesus offers eternal life.
- Jesus will never leave you the way He finds you.
- Jesus practices the law of love.

Jesus *transforms* lives!

9

WHEN WHAT YOU HAVE ISN'T ENOUGH:

Feeding the Five Thousand

MATTHEW 14:13–21; MARK 6:33–44; LUKE 9:11–17; JOHN 6:2–14

When my basket is empty and my well runs dry, it is always Jesus who can satisfy!

—Debbie Dupuy

There are times in life when what you have just isn't enough. That truth was reinforced when I invited some friends for dinner. My friend Patty loves brussels sprouts, and since I was preparing them from a recipe she had given me, I decided to invite her and her husband to dinner. I did this completely on a whim, not realizing that I wasn't preparing enough for five adults. But I didn't stop to consider the amount of food I had; I just invited them.

First, I didn't have veggies to accompany the main dish, so I quickly ran to the grocery store and bought a bag of coleslaw mix to serve as a side item. I also bought another package of brussels sprouts to ensure everyone had a full serving. Since I invited them on the spur of the moment, I only had about an hour to get everything ready. When I almost had everything in order, I received a text message from Patty asking if she could bring her daughter. I started to panic when I realized that I would be serving six people rather than five. What I had just wasn't enough.

- I had not taken the time to plan ahead.
- I had not stopped to consider if I had enough food for everyone I would be serving.
- I felt panic when I realized I did not have enough.

Do you have experiences like mine? You suddenly realize that what you have is not enough for the need. When you figure out that your needs are much bigger than what you have or what you can accomplish on your own, you might feel overwhelmed and ready to panic. You might find yourself in one of the following situations:

- It's time to pay the insurance, and you don't have enough money.
- Your debit card is denied in a busy checkout line.
- The gas tank is empty but you take a chance, only to realize you should not take chances on empty gas tanks.
- You have been caring for a sick relative while trying to meet the demands of your own family, hold down a job, and continue your church activities. And then you wonder why you don't have enough energy to do all you need to do.
- Your nerves are on edge because a loved one is making a wrong choice. You have pleaded and reasoned to no avail.
- What you have just isn't enough.

 Feed Them!

Even Jesus' disciples were caught short. "You feed them!" He said, but the task was impossible—for men. But in God's hand, "nothing" can become "everything," and "not much" can be "plenty."

The feeding of the five thousand men is the only miracle recorded in all four Gospel accounts. It is only one of two miracles

Jesus performed when He created something from something else. The first time, Jesus turned water into wine (John 2:1–11).

The feeding of the five thousand men is at the top of the list among my favorite Bible lessons. I like to teach this event to five-year-olds, using five wheat rolls and two plastic fish in a basket. The children are always excited about opening the basket and looking inside. One little boy once said as he peered inside that basket, "You mean that's all Jesus had to feed all those people? Five little rolls and two plastic fish?"

You should have heard how I explained that one. The wonder of children is amazing when it comes to Jesus. They love Him. They easily believe what the Bible says about Him, and they readily accept those teachings. Oh, how I wish we adults could be that accepting of Him.

Come aside by yourselves to a deserted place and rest a while.

The Background

The feeding of the five thousand men was at the beginning of Jesus' third year of ministry. He had performed many miracles, including turning water into wine and healing lepers and paralytics. He had also raised a widow's son from the dead, stilled a storm, and cast out demons.

The Twelve had been with Jesus for three years. He had sent them out to perform many of the kinds of miracles they had seen Him perform (Mark 6:7–13, 30; Luke 9:1–6, 10).

Can you imagine how the Twelve must have felt when they performed miracles? I can almost feel their anticipation as they looked forward to returning to Jesus to tell Him all they had done. Maybe Peter and John said, "We can't wait to tell Him that we too cast out demons." Or maybe Andrew and James couldn't wait to tell Him how they had brought life back into the body of a dead child.

But while they were performing miracles, the news came that John the Baptist had been beheaded. "When [John's] disciples heard of it, they came and took away his corpse and laid it in a tomb" (Mark 6:14–29).

At a time when Jesus' disciples were performing miracles, they found that one they loved had died a tragic death. Stop and think of the emotional exhaustion that must have followed when, at the end of such a long day, the disciples were faced with assisting Jesus in feeding an enormous gathering of people.

And He said to them, "Come aside by yourselves to a deserted place and rest a while" . . . But the multitudes saw them departing, and many knew Him and ran there on foot from all the cities. They arrived before them and came together to Him. And Jesus, when He came out, saw a great multitude and was moved with compassion for them, because they were like sheep not having a shepherd. So He began to teach them many things. When the day was now far spent, His disciples came to Him and said, "This is a deserted place, and already the hour is late. Send them away, that they may go into the surrounding country and villages and buy themselves bread; for they have nothing to eat."

But He answered and said to them, "You give them something to eat."

And they said to Him, "Shall we go and buy two hundred denarii worth of bread and give them something to eat?"

But He said to them, "How many loaves do you have? Go and see."

And when they found out they said, "Five, and two fish." . . .

And when He had taken the five loaves and the two fish, He looked up to heaven, blessed and broke the loaves, and gave them to His

Make them sit down in groups of fifty.

disciples to set before them; and the two fish He divided among them all. So they all ate and were filled. And they took up twelve baskets full of fragments and of the fish. Now those who had eaten the loaves were about five thousand men (Mark 6:31–44).

▌▌ Underline the "action words" in Jesus' red-letter text (Mark 6:30–44).

▌▌ From your own red-letter Bible, read aloud John's account of the feeding miracle (John 6:1–14). Compare John's account with Mark's account (Mark 6:30–44).

▌▌ What are the red-letter action words in John's account? Write them here.

▌▌ Why did Jesus ask His disciples, "Where shall we buy bread, that these may eat?" (John 6:5).

▌▌ Which disciple said, "There is a lad here who has five barley loaves and two small fish" (John 6:8–9)? Why do you think he said this to Jesus? Could he have been pointing out their lack of food for such a large crowd?

▌▌ How did Jesus respond to Andrew's observation?

▌▌ What is the first thing Jesus did when He took the loaves (Mark 6:41)?

📖 What do you suppose happened to the disciples' faith as they saw the five loaves and two fish being multiplied?

_____

Jesus' miracle was witnessed by a very large crowd, upward of fifteen thousand people. The Bible gives us only the number of men, but since Passover was near, women and children were accompanying the men (John 6:4; Matthew 14:21). It would stand to reason that each man had a wife, and if they had two children, the numbers could have been twenty thousand. But no matter what number we may assume, the crowd was large. We're going to play it safe and call it fifteen thousand.

❤️ Crowd-Feeding by a Prophet

Can you imagine fifteen thousand people showing up for dinner at your house? Probably not. But if it happened, and you have emojicons on your iPhone, you would be texting all of your friends the one with the "bugged-out" eyes. I think I would!

Feeding that multitude has many similarities to an Old Testament account of bread being multiplied. Perhaps when Jesus feeds the crowd of fifteen thousand, He is calling their minds to another time when one of God's prophets feeds a large crowd of people (2 Kings 4:42–44).

📖 Read 2 Kings 4:42–44 aloud and summarize that miracle of a little bread and a lot of leftovers.

_____

📖 What is the global lesson of God's ability?

_____

📖 How do we often question God's sufficiency?

_____

Impossible without God

Jesus told the disciples to give the people something to eat. When He asked them, *"How much do you have?"* He was drawing their attention to the fact that they didn't have enough. Andrew had reported that a boy in the crowd had five barley loaves and two small fish (John 6:8–9). In other words, Andrew was saying, "This is hardly enough to feed all these people."

The crowd was so large that, according to Philip, even eight months' salary—two hundred denarii—wouldn't be enough to feed them. For us today, it would be like going to every Walmart, major grocery chain, and local grocery store and buying all the bread they have to feed that many people at one sitting. Do you see their quandary?

How many loaves do you have? Go and see.

Barley was a common food for the poor. The well-to-do preferred wheat bread. The fish were probably dried or preserved, perhaps even pickled. There is no way that a "happy meal" with two fish nuggets and some bread would ever be enough to feed fifteen thousand people. Excuse me, that is fifteen thousand people—minimum! The disciples probably thought, *It is impossible for us to feed all these people!* And it was—without God.

What we must keep in mind is that Jesus already knew what He was going to do. He is about to teach them once again that no matter what the problem is, He will supply the solution. The disciples saw a lack of food, but Jesus saw a lack of faith.

On what were the disciples focusing?

107

📖 On what were Andrew and Philip focusing, rather than the solution?

_____

📖 On what occasion or occasions have you misdirected your focus as Andrew and Philip did?

_____

📖 Instead of a lack of food, what did Jesus see in the disciples?

_____

📖 How meaningful is Luke 1:37 to you? Write it here.

_____

💜 By His Hand

I love what Matthew records as Jesus turns the spotlight upon His disciples: "You give them something to eat," they reply, "We have here only five loaves and two fish." Then Jesus says, "Bring them here to Me" (Matthew 14:16–18).

The disciples do not seem to comprehend who their teacher is. Sadly, many today have the same dilemma. The demands of life can be so overwhelming that we focus on our problems rather than God's solution. The lesson for us is that no matter what we are facing, He will provide. What are you facing?

- A loveless marriage?
- A growing stack of unpaid bills?
- A diagnosis you don't understand?
- A strained relationship that only you are willing to mend?

- A situation beyond your control that has left you feeling frustrated and discouraged?

- An unrepentant prodigal child?

As Jesus stated, "With men this is impossible, but with God all things are possible" (Matthew 19:26). When God gets involved, amazing solutions can happen. The poem, "It Depends on Whose Hands It's In" by Paul Cinirag illustrates the sentiment that we must learn by placing everything in His hands. Here are a few words: "Two fish and five loaves of bread in my hands is a couple of fish sandwiches. Two fish and five loaves of bread in Jesus' hands will feed thousands; it depends whose hands it's in."

If you have faith as a mustard seed, . . . nothing will be impossible for you.

Before Jesus began to feed the people on the mountainside, He paused and gave thanks to God for supplying their needs. As Jesus looked up to heaven, a common practice in the Jewish culture, He blessed and broke the loaves. Although the Gospel writers do not record Jesus' prayer as He blessed the bread, the traditional Jewish blessing was brief and simple: "Blessed art Thou, Lord our God, King of the world, who bringeth forth bread from the earth." Each Gospel writer includes Jesus' blessing the bread before He distributed it to the crowd.

▌▌ What is Jesus teaching us about being thankful for what God provides?

▌▌ How do you feel about praying before a meal? Is it a tradition or something Christ shows us we should do? Discuss.

Compassion, and Comfort

When Jesus took these five small loaves of bread and two small fish to feed such a large crowd, He was showing His power and rule over creation. He was also showing His compassion on them; they were like sheep not having a shepherd. Jesus looks at us with the same compassion. He cares about our physical needs as well as our emotional and spiritual needs. In fact, Jesus tells us not to worry because our heavenly Father is well aware of all that we need. We can trust Him.

📖 Read Jesus' words in Matthew 6:25–34. Why does Jesus tell us not to worry?

_____

📖 Find other passages in Scripture that mention worry. What commands are we given about worry?

_____

📖 How are you measuring up to those commands?

_____

Jesus wanted the disciples (and us) to learn that God is a God of abundance. There is no reason to worry when we put our needs into His hands. He will always provide. When Jesus fed the fifteen thousand, there was more than enough food. In fact, they had leftovers.

So when they were filled, He said to His disciples, "Gather up the fragments that remain, so that nothing is lost." Therefore they gathered them up, and filled twelve baskets with the fragments of the five barley loaves which were left over by those who had eaten (John 6:12–13).

> *Filled,* in the Greek language, has two meanings: "to fill completely" and "fatted"; that is, pig out.

Jesus reveals that He is more than enough. In comparison, the people were about to experience an elaborate feast during Passover. Jesus' feast consisted of five small loaves of bread and two dried fish, a meager sack lunch that left everyone completely full. Paul said, "And my God shall supply all your need according to His riches in glory by Christ Jesus" (Philippians 4:19).

His hands are capable; in fact, He created the universe. "All things were made through Him, and without Him nothing was made that was made" (John 1:3).

When Jesus comes in and fills our deepest needs, there is always something left to draw upon.

> The Lord will guide you continually,
> And satisfy your soul in drought,
> And strengthen your bones;
> You shall be like a watered garden,
> And like a spring of water, whose waters do not fail.
>
> —Isaiah 58:11

Life with Jesus is a continuous fountain, always satisfying our deepest needs. His life flows through us, even when we feel as if we are not enough or that we don't have enough to satisfy our needs. Jesus is always enough. With Him our cup overflows like a continuous running fountain (Psalm 23:5).

 The Great I Am

The Gospels are all about affirmations. Jesus revealed Himself as the Lord over all creation when He walked on water, calmed a storm,

Most assuredly, I say to you, before Abraham was, I AM.

and fed thousands with the grain He created. But of all the affirmations in the Gospels concerning Jesus, the one question He continually asks is: "Who do you say that I am?

Jesus proclaims with every miracle, *I am the Lord! I am the Messiah!*

In *Jesus: A Theography,* Leonard Sweet and Frank Viola point out that "in the Jewish mind, sickness was caused by one's own sin. They believed that the Messiah would cleanse lepers, cast out demons, and heal blindness. These three were regarded as Messianic."[20]

The following scriptures show that Jesus proved what the Jews were said to believe but rejected: Matthew 12:22–23; Luke 5:17; 7:20–22; John 7:2–5; Acts 2:22.

Jesus fulfilled every Old Testament prophecy regarding Himself: Isaiah 42:1–3; 52:2–13; Daniel 9:24–27; Micah 5:2; Zechariah 9:9; and others.

He satisfied the roles as a prophet, priest, and king, all three pointing to the fact that He was the Messiah.

📖 Who do you say that He is?

_____

📖 What do you believe He can do?

_____

📖 If Jesus can feed fifteen thousand people with only five loaves of bread and two small fish, what can He do for you?

_____

When the odds are overwhelming and you are faced with something unimaginable, how can Jesus help you handle it?

Even though Jesus fed that enormous crowd, He knew that physical bread satisfies for only a few short hours. Then people are hungry again. Jesus later explains:

- "I am the bread of life. He who comes to Me shall never hunger, and he who believes in Me shall never thirst" (John 6:35).

- "I am the bread which came down from heaven" (John 6:41).

- "I am the bread of life" (John 6:48).

- "Your fathers ate the manna in the wilderness, and are dead. This is the bread which comes down from heaven, that one may eat of it and not die. I am the living bread which came down from heaven. If anyone eats of this bread, he will live forever; and the bread that I shall give is My flesh, which I shall give for the life of the world" (John 6:49–51).

Jesus makes a connection between physical bread and spiritual bread. While the physical bread temporarily fills the stomach, those who follow Jesus will never be empty. Spiritual bread is always satisfying. All the following statements relate to John 6:35:

- By equating Himself with bread, Jesus is saying He is essential for life.

- The life to which Jesus is referring is not physical but eternal. He gave the multitude physical bread that perishes. He is spiritual bread that brings eternal life.

- Jesus is making another claim to deity. This statement is the first of the "I AM" statements in John's Gospel. The phrase "I AM" is the covenant name of God (Yahweh or YHWH) revealed to

Moses at the burning bush (Exodus 3:14). The Jews understood that as a claim to deity.

Closely related to Jesus' proclamation in John 6:35 is this beatitude: "Blessed are those who hunger and thirst for righteousness, for they shall be filled" (Matthew 5:6). When Jesus says those who come to Him will never hunger and those who believe in Him will never thirst, He is saying that He will satisfy our hunger and thirst to be made righteous in the sight of God.

What Did You Learn?

1 Jesus was teaching the disciples that God will always supply more than we need.

2 Jesus can take something small and insignificant and do great things with it, if we are willing to give it to Him. After all, we must not forget that the little boy in the crowd was willing to give his lunch to Jesus. If he had not been willing, he would not have participated in Jesus' blessings.

3 Jesus could have made just enough, but He wanted to show that there is abundance when we follow Him. Each disciple had his own basket. Jesus was revealing, "I will provide for you."

4 In Jesus' hands, there is always enough; even leftovers.

THE WORLD'S BEST BRUSSELS SPROUTS RECIPE

(given to me by my friend Patty)

Ingredients

Kosher salt and freshly ground black pepper
4 cups whole brussels sprouts
8 slices molasses-cured shoulder bacon or regular bacon
6 cloves garlic, chopped

Directions

Fill a large saucepan with water, add a pinch of salt, and bring to a boil. Add the brussels sprouts and cook them for about 8 minutes. Remove the sprouts from the heat, drain, and then chill them in the refrigerator. (I blanche them in cold water and return them to the pan.) Slice the sprouts in half when they have cooled. (I leave them whole.)

In a large skillet, cook the bacon over medium heat until it is done. (I cut the bacon into little pieces before frying.) Discard all but 2 tablespoons of bacon fat and grease from the pan, leaving the 2 tablespoons in the pan. Add the garlic and cook for a few minutes over medium-low heat until fragrant. Add the sprouts and cook until heated through. Season the sprouts with kosher salt and fresh black pepper, to taste. Enjoy.

HE'LL FIND YOU IN THE HURRICANE!

Jesus Walks on the Sea

MATTHEW 14:22–33

Jesus is the reason that I can get up every morning and face the challenges of the day. He is the One who gives me the courage to face the darkest storms.

—Debbie Dupuy

Have you ever had a day that seemed to go from bad to worse within a short amount of time? I am reminded of the children's story by Judith Viorst, *Alexander and the Terrible, Horrible, No Good, Very Bad Day.* Alexander woke up with gum in his hair—and it got worse. His best friend deserted him. There was no dessert in his lunch bag. And, on top of all that, there were lima beans for dinner and kissing on TV!

I, too, have experienced days like Alexander's, as we all have, days when it seems as though things go from bad to worse in less time than it takes to microwave a cup of coffee. During these times we need solutions to help us get through "terrible, horrible, no good, very bad days."

Snowball Effect

For several years I faced so many obstacles that I began to feel as though I were drowning. The reason I remember those times so vividly is because I decided to write down every bad thing that had happened to me or my family within the course of one year. By the time I finished the list, I had filled a notebook page—twenty-seven lines, in case you are wondering.

I felt pounded by the waves of anxiety, exhaustion, worry, and fear. Everything seemed to happen in succession, one event after another. You know those times. You're in the midst of an unfortunate event and before it's over, another problem raises its head. What Alexander was experiencing and what I experienced is the snowball effect. As a snowball rolls down the mountainside, it gains speed, but it also gathers snow. By the time it reaches the bottom, it has grown to an enormous size. And so are life's negative circumstances. Life's difficulties keep bombarding us until our snowball reaches a size so enormous we cannot handle it.

It's during these seasons of life that we have to take the hand of Jesus and let Him pull us to safety. We may have problems, but Jesus is always the solution.

📖 Share a time when you had a terrible, horrible, no good, very bad day.

Before the Storm

When we study the Scriptures, it is imperative that we visualize the characters as real people with the same feelings we have. The disciples are no exception. As the events leading up to Jesus' walking on water unfolded, the disciples' emotions were frazzled. They were exhausted and overwhelmed. It seems that throughout the course of

118

their day, they had experienced the snowball effect. Look at their rolling snowball:

- They learn about the death of John the Baptist.
- Perhaps they are saddened by the cruelty of his death and public display of his severed head on a platter.
- They might sympathize with the task of John's disciples in the preparation and burial of their teacher.
- They probably grieve the loss with Jesus.
- Jesus sees a great multitude and begins healing the sick.
- Evening approaches and the disciples are ready to end their day.
- Jesus decides to feed about fifteen thousand people, and they are included in the largest fish fry in history.

Peace I leave with you; My peace I give you.

Afterward, He told His disciples to get into a boat and go to Bethsaida. He then sent the multitude away and went upon the mountain to pray. The disciples might have shared some of Alexander's thinking: *This has been a terrible, horrible, no good, very bad day!*

They experienced the snowball effect that day. None of us have ever experienced the trauma of a friend's being beheaded or the need to feed fifteen thousand at one sitting. I wonder if the disciples were thinking, *We can finally get some rest.* And yet another unforeseen circumstance surfaces—a life-threatening storm in the middle of the night.

📖 Make a quick review of Matthew 14:1–21, and discuss the disciples' physical exhaustion as well as the emotional trauma they had experienced that day. What must they have been feeling?

_____

📖 What does this reveal about Jesus' compassion for people, even though He is heartbroken and tired?

_____

📖 Why is it difficult to maintain that kind of compassion when we are hurting?

_____

💜 A Storm Rocks the Boat

Immediately Jesus made His disciples get into the boat and go before Him to the other side, while He sent the multitudes away. And when He had sent the multitudes away, He went up on the mountain by Himself to pray. Now when evening came, He was alone there. But the boat was now in the middle of the sea, tossed by the waves, for the wind was contrary. Now in the fourth watch of the night Jesus went to them, walking on the sea. And when the disciples saw Him walking on the sea, they were troubled, saying, "It is a ghost!" And they cried out for fear (Matthew 14:22–26).

The disciples found themselves in the middle of the Sea of Galilee in a terrible storm around three in the morning. I wonder if, during that hurricane-like storm, they were screaming for help. Maybe they were yelling to one another about what to do to keep the boat afloat. Did they lose their footing on the deck and cling to any stationary object they could find as they were being tossed around like a tin can on the sea?

Now picture this. The disciples are rowing, trying to survive the tempest, and they notice a figure bobbing up and down in the distance. Then they cry out, "It's a ghost!" They are even more frightened.

📖 Describe the pictures you have seen of Jesus as He walked on the water.

_____

📖 Have you always pictured Jesus as walking calmly toward the boat?

_____

📖 Describe the fear the disciples experienced as they saw their Lord walking on the stormy sea.

_____

💜 The Creator on the Water

For now forget the pictures you have seen of Jesus as he walked on the water. Artists have depicted Him on water that is almost still and serene. That's not the picture the Bible paints. A storm was unleashing its full force. Matthew says "the wind was boisterous" (Matthew 14:30). As the disciples watched the figure of a man coming toward them, it probably looked as though He was bobbing up and down, because Jesus was rising and falling with the motion of the waves. And the waves were climbing to great heights and then crashing down. However, this was the Creator of the universe walking through the storm. They watched as Jesus was blown by the powerful winds, and as He rode the pounding waves on His way toward them. They were sure it was a ghost, as they cried out in fear.

But immediately Jesus spoke to them, saying, "Be of good cheer! It is I; do not be afraid" (Matthew 14:27).

When Peter realizes the figure is Jesus, he asks Him if he, too, can walk on water. But as Peter walks toward Jesus—on water, I remind you—he gets sidetracked by the boisterous winds and takes his eyes off Jesus. He begins to sink. Jesus stretches out His loving arms and saves Peter in the storm. Jesus is revealing to Peter a valuable lesson about trusting Him.

What Did Jesus Reveal about Himself During the Storm?

Jesus' walking on the water is a famous account of His miraculous power. It shows us a picture of who Jesus really is. Every time we read of Jesus' performing a miracle, such as raising the dead, healing incurable diseases, or taking control of nature, Jesus is revealing who He is and what He can do. Notice Jesus' words to Peter: "Be of good cheer! It is I; do not be afraid." The words of Jesus here have a deeper meaning.

Mark's account gives us something the other two accounts do not: "He came to them, walking on the sea, and would have passed them by" (Mark 6:48).

📖 What is Mark revealing about Jesus?

_____

📖 Why would Jesus want to pass them by?

_____

Matthew 14:27 and Mark 6:50 reveal these words of Jesus: "It is I." When Jesus made this statement, He was saying, "I am God in the flesh." He was proclaiming His divinity. They would have heard the words, *Be joyful, get excited, I AM WHO I AM is here. Do not be afraid!*

We must not forget that the disciples had been struggling to understand who Jesus was and why He came. They understood He was from God, but they didn't understand He was God. Jesus revealed Himself as God when He walked on the water.

When our terrible, horrible, no good, very bad days take their toll on us, we need to remember who has control—Jesus!

> For in Him dwells all the fullness of the Godhead bodily; and you are complete in Him, who is the head of all principality and power (Colossians 2:9–10).

> But thanks be to God, who gives us victory through our Lord Jesus Christ (1 Corinthians 15:57).

- Jesus is the fullness of God.

- I am complete in Him.

- He is the head of every principality and power. That means He has control over any unseen forces as well as powers on the earth.

- I have victory through Jesus Christ.

Get Out of the Boat

> And Peter answered Him and said, "Lord, if it is You, command me to come to You on the water." So He said, "Come." And when Peter had come down out of the boat, he walked on the water to go to Jesus. But when he saw that the wind was boisterous, he was afraid; and beginning to sink he cried out, saying, "Lord, save me!" (Matthew 14:28–30).

This is where most people start to talk about Peter's lack of faith. Not me.

Peter was the only one of the Twelve who got out of the boat. He deserves a standing ovation for his courage. At least he had enough faith to get out of the boat in the middle of a hurricane-like storm and attempt to walk on water. Peter was willing. He left his comfort zone. Would you have done that?

As for me, I know I would have never made such a request. Had I been commanded to walk out on water, I would have probably said, "Are you talking to me? You want me to get out of this boat and walk on water? Oh, no! Not me!"

When Jesus told Peter to come, He was testing Peter's faith. And Peter actually attempted to walk to Jesus. The other eleven stayed put. They did not call out to Jesus. They were afraid; they did not attempt anything. Peter looked to Jesus, instead of submitting to fear, and got out of that boat.

When circumstances beyond our control confront us, we need to think of Peter's willingness to go toward Jesus in a raging storm. It takes courage and faith to attempt what is next to impossible. As long as Peter kept his eyes on Jesus, he walked. But then he started operating with a logical human mindset: *I am a human being and I am walking on water; humans do not walk on water.* But then look what happened. It was almost as if he were saying, *I'm stupid. I can't walk on water. Why am I trying to do this?* It was then that Peter yelled, "Lord, save me!"

📖 What indicates that it took great faith for Peter to get out of the boat?

📖 How can we relate Peter's willingness to get out of the boat to our being stuck in a spiritual comfort zone?

📖 What comfort zone is holding you in the boat?

> And immediately Jesus stretched out His hand and caught him, and said to him, "O you of little faith, why did you doubt?" And

when they got into the boat, the wind ceased. Then those who were in the boat came and worshiped Him, saying, "Truly You are the Son of God" (Matthew 14:31–33).

Jesus' words to Peter echo in my mind: *"O you of little faith, why did you doubt?"* Hadn't Peter and the rest of the disciples heard Jesus when He said, *"It is I"*? They must have clearly understood Jesus' message: *I am God in the flesh. I can handle this storm.*

 Doubting Sinks Your Boat

Doubting and storms go hand in hand. When we face the storms of life, whether physical, emotional, financial, or in relationships with others, doubt will cause us to sink. Hebrews 12:2 reminds us to look "unto Jesus, the author and finisher of our faith." Faith is the ability to see with "kingdom eyes." When we face the storms of life, we must remember that every wave, storm, or crashing situation can actually help us move closer to Jesus. Peter's storm threw him into the hands of Jesus. If you look with kingdom eyes at your storm, it will bring you closer to the Lord.

Too often when we are faced with many trials, obstacles, and heartbreaking circumstances, we forget the one who has us in the palm of His hand. And like Peter, it's easy to lose our focus and start to doubt.

Doubting leads to the inward chatter of our minds, and inward chatter can snowball. And when you find yourself in the middle of a storm, it is easy to allow your mind to wander. The more intense a crisis becomes, the more you think about what is wrong and what can happen. And the more you worry and fret over the situation, the more you encourage the inward chatter of your

Whatever you ask in prayer, believe that you have received it.

mind to take control. Inward chatter also increases when you begin to imagine scenarios: what you believe people are thinking, what can happen, what is wrong instead of what is right. Before you realize it, you believe the lie your own mind is telling you. When inward chatter takes over, doubt arises. When we listen to inward chatter, we are opening ourselves to the enemy. Satan wants us to keep our focus on our "storm" and not on Jesus. Remember, Peter looked at his circumstances instead of looking at the Savior.

Come, be of good cheer! It is I; do not be afraid.

Anything you obsess over is a stronghold. A stronghold is an incorrect thinking pattern that has molded itself into your way of thinking. Doubt, worry, and obsessive thinking are like a rocking chair. You move but go nowhere. Negative thinking accomplishes nothing.

> For the weapons of our warfare are not carnal but mighty in God for pulling down strongholds, casting down arguments and every high thing that exalts itself against the knowledge of God, bringing every thought into captivity to the obedience of Christ (2 Corinthians 10:4–5).

I am encouraged to step out of the boat by the words of Charles H. Spurgeon: "I have learned to kiss the waves that throw me up against the Rock of Ages." Jesus is the Rock that can handle the waves of life. He is the one on whom you need to look when the waves come crashing down upon you.

Remember, as long as he focused on Jesus, Peter walked. When he focused on his circumstances, he sank. When you take your eyes off Jesus, what happens to your relationships? When you turn your focus from Jesus, what happens to the work of the church? If you stop looking to Jesus, what happens to your spiritual life?

📖 Jesus said to Peter, "O you of little faith, why did you doubt?" Place your name in that text instead of the word "you." Why *do* you sometimes doubt Him?

📖 As long as Peter was focused on Jesus, he walked, but when he looked at the boisterous waves, he lost his focus. How does this sometimes happen to you spiritually?

📖 When you feel yourself doubting and sinking, how can you remember to cast your eyes on Jesus?

Your faith will be made strong when you keep your eyes on Jesus. As we have learned, Jesus has the power over all things. Is there anything He cannot do? Many situations are too big for us to handle, but nothing is too big for Jesus.

Water-Walking Faith

When you know Jesus, you know that you can trust Him. When you keep your focus on His power, you will have the confidence to realize that He can take any storm you are facing and pull you to safety. Just as He reached with outstretched arms to Peter, He reached with outstretched arms on the cross to save us all. "O you of little faith, why do you doubt?" "Come, be of good cheer! It is I: do not be afraid."

- "You are of God, little children, and have overcome them [false prophets] because He who is in you is greater than he who is in the world" (1 John 4:4).

- "No temptation has overtaken you except such as is common to man; but God is faithful, who will not allow you to be tempted beyond what you are able, but with the temptation will also make the way of escape, that you may be able to bear it" (1 Corinthians 10:13).

- "Looking unto Jesus, the author and finisher of our faith, who for the joy that was set before Him endured the cross, despising the shame, and has sat down at the right hand of the throne of God" (Hebrews 12:2).

- "I will never leave you nor forsake you." So we may boldly say, "The Lord is my helper; I will not fear. What can man do to me?" (Hebrews 13:5–6).

Robert E. Webber, author of *Ancient-Future Worship*, relates the following story about the essence of faith:

I was flying from San Francisco to Los Angeles when I entered into a conversation with a man of Eastern descent on the subject of faith. "Tell me," I asked, "What is a good one-liner that captures the essence of your faith?"

"Sure," he said and quickly responded with these words: "We are all part of the problem. We are all part of the solution."

"Would you like to hear a Christian one-liner?" I asked.

"Well, yes, of course," he answered.

"We are all part of the problem," I said, pausing long enough for the connection to be made. "But," I added, "there is only one man who is the solution. His name is Jesus."[21]

So step out in the raging storms of life. Call His name. He'll find you in the hurricane.

The Lord your God in your midst, the Mighty One, will save; He will rejoice over you with gladness, He will quiet you with His love, He will rejoice over you with singing (Zephaniah 3:17).

GOOD DIRT— IT'S A MATTER OF THE HEART: The Sower

LUKE 8:4–15; MATTHEW 13:1–23; MARK 4:3–20

But the ones [the seed] that fell on the good ground
are those who, having heard the word with a noble
and good heart, keep it and bear fruit with patience.

—Luke 8:15

The love of gardening is in my blood. My love for getting my hands in the dirt goes back to my great-grandmother, Mamma Garrard. When I was but a young girl, she took me deep into the woods with a bucket and shovel to find "good dirt." After walking for a short time, I'd hear her say, "Stop right here. This is the good dirt." Then we began pulling back old leaves and limbs until we found that rich black dirt she sought.

"That's the good dirt," Mamma Garrard would say. "Now, you have to smell it. Go on, take a sniff."

"Take a sniff of what?" I asked.

She replied, "The good dirt, of course."

Then I argued, "I don't want to smell the dirt. Who smells dirt anyway?"

She would have no part of it, I had to smell the dirt. In fact, we couldn't begin shoveling until I smelled its richness. She taught me the secret of growing beautiful flowers. "It's all about the dirt," she would say. I then would take a sniff. I can still smell that richness of the forest floor when I remember our times together. After that smell test, we would begin shoveling those rich nutrients into the bucket and head home.

Because of her dirt, Mamma Garrard's flowers were unsurpassed. She grew the largest impatiens I've ever seen. (She called them Sultanas.) Her flowers looked like they were on steroids, with stalks as big as half-dollars. I can hear her words still: "Debbie, just remember; it's all about the good dirt."

Four Soils for the Seed

Jesus taught about good dirt too. His red-letter words teach us about four kinds of soil. Jesus used earthly things to teach spiritual lessons that everyone could understand. That's what a parable is: an earthly story with a spiritual meaning. Understanding a parable is like peeling an apple. The skin is the story itself, the meat is the context, and the core is the spiritual application.

Let's listen as Jesus describes four kinds of soils in a parable:

> "A sower went out to sow his seed. And as he sowed, some fell by the wayside; and it was trampled down, and the birds of the air devoured it. Some fell on rock; and as soon as it sprang up, it withered away because it lacked moisture. And some fell among thorns, and the thorns sprang up with it and choked it. But others fell on good ground, sprang up, and yielded a crop a hundredfold." **When He had said these things He cried,** "He who has ears to hear, let him hear!" **Then His disciples asked Him, saying,** "What does this parable mean?" **And He said,** "To you it has been given to know the mysteries of the kingdom of God, but to the rest it is given in parables, that 'Seeing they may not see, and hearing they may not understand'" (Luke 8:5–10).

Anytime Jesus says, "He who has ears to hear, let him hear," He is challenging us to pay careful attention. He wants us to listen with spiritual ears and glean the spiritual truths from His teaching. He is asking us to listen with the ears of our heart. (I bet you didn't know your heart has ears. Well, it does.)

Jesus makes this challenging statement again in Revelation 2:7: "He who has an ear, let him hear what the Spirit says to the churches. To him who overcomes I will give to eat from the tree of life, which is in the midst of the Paradise of God."

Jesus is saying, "Listen up! Take notice! Pay attention!"

 A Good-Dirt Heart

Jesus begins to explain the parable:

> Now the parable is this: The seed is the word of God. Those by the wayside are the ones who hear; then the devil comes and takes away the word out of their hearts, lest they should believe and be saved. But the ones on the rock are those who, when they hear, receive the word with joy; and these have no root, who believe for a while and in time of temptation fall away. Now the ones that fell among thorns are those who, when they have heard, go out and are choked with cares, riches, and pleasures of life, and bring no fruit to maturity. But the ones that fell on the good ground are those who, having heard the word with a noble and good heart, keep it and bear fruit with patience (Luke 8:11–15).

The heart is of utmost importance to God. "For the Lord does not see as a man sees; for man looks at the outward appearance, but the Lord looks at the heart" (1 Samuel 16:7). God knows what is in your heart. He knows the depth of your heart and how you are cultivating it for life or destruction.

Jesus explains that the Word of God is planted in the heart, but the outcome depends on the kind of heart into which it falls.

📖 According to Jesus' explanation, what is the seed?

_____

📖 List each type of soil and the fate of the seed that fell there.

_____

Since most of Jesus' audience were farmers, they understood His descriptions of soil. They understood the challenges of growing wheat and barley in a dusty, rocky countryside. They knew that good soil made all the difference. However, the larger picture is the spiritual application of the soils.

HARD HEART—BY THE WAYSIDE

The first heart is an unresponsive heart, a hard heart. Here's a glimpse of the "spiritual forces of evil" at work.

> Having their understanding darkened, being alienated from the life of God, because of the ignorance that is in them, because of the blindness of their heart (Ephesians 4:18).

Perhaps hardheartedness happens when the Word of God cuts one to the heart sharply, enabling an understanding of what one should and should not do. However, some individuals might not want to know what the Word of God says, because they do not want to make decisions based upon it. Regardless, when the Word of God is heard or taught to someone with a hard heart, Jesus relates it to the path in the field, a place by the wayside. This path had been packed hard by the feet of farmers going to and from the field. The audience understood that the seed that fell there could not sink into the soil. It would be only bird feed.

"The devil comes and takes away the word out of their hearts, lest they believe and be saved" (Luke 8:12). Notice who is at work when a hardhearted individual hears the powerful Word of God. Satan is ready and waiting to accommodate the hardened heart. He snatches the Word away before it has a chance to sink in.

132

Make no mistake here, anytime the Word is presented to unbelievers, Satan gets to work on their rejection statements. You must remember, the unbelievers are not rejecting you but they are rejecting the Word of God. Determine in your own heart to pray for them and seek other opportunities to teach and influence them. Nothing makes me happier than knowing the devil has been defeated by the powerful, living Word of God.

> For the word of God is living and powerful and sharper than any two-edged sword, piercing as far as the separation of the soul and spirit, joints and marrow. It is able to judge the ideas and thoughts of the heart (Hebrews 4:12).

How long did Satan wait before snatching the Word from the hardhearted (Mark 4:15)?

How does knowing that Satan is at work help you?

It is interesting to note that the next three soils represent the hearts of those who have received the seed, but only one soil produces a crop.

SHALLOW HEART—ON THE ROCKS

In this instance, the Word gets into the heart, but it has no chance of producing fruit. The hearer is delighted by the Word, but when troubles come, his shallow heart cannot properly process his trials. The seed sprouts and grows a little, but because of the underlying rock bed, it never develops a nourishing root system, so it cannot get the nutrients that would otherwise sustain it. That kind of heart never develops a relationship with God. People with rocky-soil hearts wilt at the first discouragement or obstacle to their faith and allow the trials and frustrations of life to pull them away from God. Note Jesus' words as related by two inspired men, Mark and Luke:

But the ones on the rock are those who, when they hear, receive the word with joy; and these have no root, who believe for a while and in time of temptation fall away (Luke 8:13).

These likewise are the ones sown on stony ground who, when they hear the word, immediately receive it with gladness; and they have no root in themselves, and so endure only for a time. Afterward, when tribulation or persecution arises for the word's sake, immediately they stumble (Mark 4:16–17).

I have seen rocky-soil hearts many times. Several of my acquaintances have experienced a series of unfortunate events in their lives. They start missing worship and Bible study occasionally. Then as the problems intensify, which always happens when God is rejected, they became more and more distracted. We must understand that becoming a child of God doesn't make us immune from trials. The Bible teaches repeatedly that we will have problems and difficulties in life. We are never promised a rose garden, are we?

Our lives are sometimes like that of Chippie the parakeet.

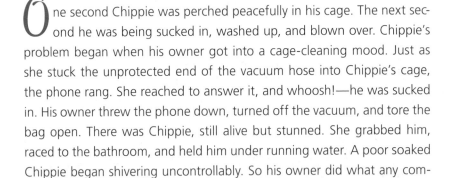

One second Chippie was perched peacefully in his cage. The next second he was being sucked in, washed up, and blown over. Chippie's problem began when his owner got into a cage-cleaning mood. Just as she stuck the unprotected end of the vacuum hose into Chippie's cage, the phone rang. She reached to answer it, and whoosh!—he was sucked in. His owner threw the phone down, turned off the vacuum, and tore the bag open. There was Chippie, still alive but stunned. She grabbed him, raced to the bathroom, and held him under running water. A poor soaked Chippie began shivering uncontrollably. So his owner did what any compassionate bird owner would do. She switched on the blow dryer and blasted him with hot air. Poor Chippie had no idea what was hitting him.

A few days after the trauma, a friend called to check on Chippie.

"Well, Chippie doesn't sing much anymore," his owner replied. "He just sits and stares."

———————————●———————————

We have to realize that as long as we have breath, we will have problems. "Man who is born of woman is of few days and full of trouble" (Job 14:1). Paul concurs with Job: "Yes, and all who desire to live godly in Christ Jesus will suffer persecution" (2 Timothy 3:12).

We are told again and again that we will suffer trials and troubles, and we shouldn't be surprised by them.

📖 How do trials and problems often affect new believers? Give examples.

_____

📖 What prevents a new believer from developing a root system?

_____

📖 Should we ever be surprised by problems in our lives? Support your answer with scripture.

_____

Why is Bible study the first step in moving rocks? Because God's Word provides solutions to our problems, and we always have problems. "Milk" is sometimes used as a metaphor to help us understand the fact that sustenance comes from the Word of God. It is like pouring fertilizer on a plant. It will produce blooms and enable us to digest "meat," which will help us develop strong root systems that will produce mature fruit. Martin Luther once said,

> The Bible is alive; it speaks to me;
> It has feet; it runs after me;
> It has hands; it lays hold of me.

When trials come, we need to allow the roots of God's Word to bury deep into our hearts that we may continue to produce fruit for Him. We must constantly associate with Christians who can encourage us and build us up during hard times.

> Beware, brethren, lest there be in any of you an evil heart of unbelief in departing from the living God: but exhort one another daily, while it is called "Today," lest any of you be hardened through the deceitfulness of sin (Hebrews 3:12–13).

I have lived long enough to know that life can change in an instant. We need to be prepared for the "what if's" of life. Shallow hearts are not prepared for deep trials.

- Suppose you get the diagnosis you feared. Then what?
- Suppose you face financial ruin. Then what?
- Suppose you get the phone call in the middle of the night that turns your world upside down. Then what?
- Suppose your child hurts and disappoints you by making an immoral choice. Then what?

What If, What If, What If? Get the Picture?

If you allow God's Word to be rooted and grounded in you, the "what if's" will not tear you away from the Lord. One who produces fruit for God knows there are over six thousand promises in His Word for His children. It would serve us well to know these promises when trials come.

- "I can do all things through Christ who strengthens me" (Philippians 4:13).
- "With God all things are possible" (Matthew 19:26).

- "Now if God so clothes the grass of the field . . . do not worry, saying, 'What shall we eat?' or 'What shall we drink?' or 'What shall we wear?'" (Matthew 6:30–31).

- "Desire the pure milk of the word, that you may grow thereby" (1 Peter 2:2).

- "Your word is a lamp to my feet and a light to my path" (Psalm 119:105).

WORLDLY HEART—AMONG THE THORNS

The worldly heart allows the world's influence to choke out the Word of God. It produces no spiritual fruit because worldliness has smothered and stifled any pursuit of a deep relationship with God.

The thorny soil describes Christians who are interested only in themselves—accumulating material things, pursuing entertainment and a worldly lifestyle—rather than serving God and reaching the lost. Worldly hearted Christians have their priorities in the wrong place. Jesus knew that. This is the result of a thorny heart: Christians who attend church each week, regularly attend Bible classes, and put some money in the collection plate but never bear any fruit. They keep their focus on themselves rather than what's eternal. God's seed fell among the thorns in their heart, and even though the seed sprouted, the plants never came to fruition because their life was choked out.

Wouldn't it be wonderful if you could just whip out your weed killer and get rid of all the worldliness around you like you kill the thorns on your lawn? In fact, some brands of weed killer are rainproof for a short time, and weeds are promised to be completely gone within six hours. It would be fantastic to spray away anything that keeps us from spending time with God or getting our priorities mixed up. Remember Jesus said in the text, "He who has ears to hear, let him hear." He meant, *Listen with your spiritual ears.* Many of us have forgotten to do that. We have become spiritually deaf. Many of us can relate to deafness because we experience it firsthand, like one woman from Alabama.

Aman and his wife were returning home to Florence, Alabama. An Arkansas State Trooper stopped them and asked the husband, "Do you know how fast you were driving?"

The wife asked her husband: "What did he say?"

The husband replied, "He asked if I knew how fast I was driving?"

The trooper looked at the man's driver's license: "I see you're not from around here."

"No," the man replied. "We are from Florence, Alabama."

The wife asked again, "What did you say?"

The husband told her in a loud voice, "I said we are from Florence, Alabama."

The state trooper commented, "Oh, wow. The meanest woman I ever met was from Florence, Alabama."

The wife asked again, "What did he say?"

The husband replied, "He thinks he knows you."

Sometimes culture affects spiritual hearing in a similar way. You can't hear because you have become spiritually deaf. You need to be reminded that Christians are called by Jesus to live differently from those around them. You must remember that we are to live according to God's values rather than human values. Notice from the following verses what our attitude toward the world should be.

> And do not be conformed to this world, but be transformed by the renewing of your mind, that you may prove what is that good and acceptable and perfect will of God (Romans 12:2).

> Do not love the world or the things in the world. If anyone loves the world, the love of the Father is not in him. For all that is in the

world—the lust of the flesh, the lust of the eyes, and the pride of life—is not of the Father but is of the world (1 John 2:15–16).

Beware lest anyone cheat you through philosophy and empty deceit, according to the tradition of men, according to the basic principles of the world, and not according to Christ (Colossians 2:8).

Anything that takes your focus from God in an unhealthy way will kill you spiritually.

■■ What kinds of worldly things take your focus from God?

_____

■■ If you could use weed killer on worldliness, what would you kill in six hours or less?

_____

■■ How has worldliness affected Christians today? The church?

_____

Sometimes we need to be reminded that Jesus made a difference between His followers and those of the world. He tells us in the parable of the soils, it is a matter of the heart. When we become a follower of Jesus, we live differently.

I have been crucified with Christ; it is no longer I who live, but Christ lives in me (Galatians 2:20).

If anyone is in Christ, he is a new creation; old things have passed away; behold all things have become new (2 Corinthians 5:17).

GOOD GROUND—THE GOOD-DIRT HEART

Jesus knows that if you will take the Word into your heart, learn it, and practice it, your life will produce fruit.

But the ones that fell on the good ground are those who, having heard the word with a noble and good heart, keep it and bear fruit with patience (Luke 8:15).

> But these are the ones sown on good ground, those who hear the word, accept it, and bear fruit: some thirtyfold, some sixty, and some a hundred (Mark 4:20).

Jesus explains to His disciples that this spiritual soil would produce much more than a normal harvest, in fact, a hundred times what was planted. This would have been unimaginable to them.

Their best crop production was from ten to twenty times what they planted. Can you imagine what they must have thought when Jesus told them that they could produce more than ten times their normal harvest? I can hear the crowd saying to Him, "Please tell us how to do this." Can you imagine the puzzled looks on their faces as Jesus presented this parable? I can see them shaking their heads in disbelief. But Jesus was describing the rich fertile grounds of the heart. He explained that a life that receives His Word, nourishes it, and tends it will produce much fruit. What is the result of a good-dirt heart? Imagine your life as a tree filled with beautiful, delicious fruit, and the purpose of your tree is so that others can come and gather the fruit of the Spirit from it.

> Love, joy, peace, longsuffering, kindness, goodness, faithfulness, gentleness, self-control (Galatians 5:22–23).

> Therefore, my brethren, you also have become dead to the law through the body of Christ, that you may be married to another— to Him who was raised from the dead, that we should bear fruit to God (Romans 7:4).

> For this reason we . . . do not cease to pray for you, and to ask that you may be filled with the knowledge of His will in all wisdom and spiritual understanding; that you may walk worthy of the Lord, fully pleasing Him, being fruitful in every good work and increasing in the knowledge of God (Colossians 1:9–10).

> Now may He who supplies seed to the sower, and bread for food, supply and multiply the seed you have sown and increase the fruits of your righteousness (2 Corinthians 9:10).

📖 What happens to the seed sown in good soil (Luke 8:15; Mark 4:20)?

_____

📖 Did you notice that "fruit of the Spirit" is singular? Why is it written that way when nine "fruits" are mentioned? Can we possess one without the other?

_____

📖 What four things does Colossians 1:10 list that good-dirt hearts possess?

_____

📖 Relate "increasing in the knowledge of God" to the seed planted in the parable.

_____

📖 How is the seed multiplied (2 Corinthians 9:10)?

_____

We can bear fruit to God in many ways because we all have different talents and abilities.

❶ Use your talents.

❷ Share your God-given gifts with others.

❸ Increase your knowledge of God.

❹ Teach someone the gospel.

Sowing and Reaping

Jesus wants full control of our hearts. He knows that a life of joy and productivity is one that bears fruit for the kingdom. These hearts take in His words. They grow, learn, and develop into something very beautiful.

141

In addition to developing the fruit of the Spirit, Paul connects our lives and hearts to sowing and reaping. There is a connection between how we live and what we do.

> Do not be deceived, God is not mocked; for whatever a man sows, that he will also reap. For he who sows to his flesh [the unspiritual part of life] will of the flesh reap corruption [as did the first three soils Jesus described], but he who sows to the Spirit will of the Spirit reap everlasting life (Galatians 6:7–8).

You see, dear friend, if your heart is pure, cultivated, and nourished with the Word of God, your life will produce a spiritual harvest for the Lord. If you weed out anything that chokes you spiritually and if you kill anything that tries to take your focus away from Jesus, you will produce not only what is expected in the parable—ten to twenty times the amount planted—but also exceedingly more than you could ever imagine, a hundred times the amount you plant. Jesus wants you to get that. He wants you to know that your heart is very important in the production of spiritual fruit, but it has to be filled, cultivated, and planted with Him.

Remember my great-grandmother's impatiens, her flowers so full of blooms that their branches were weighed down? I can still see her front porch lined with pots and buckets of flowers with the most colorful blooms—bright red, fuchsia, and brilliant orange. However, Mamma Garrard never used Miracle Grow. People were amazed at her beautiful flowers and often asked her, "Victoria, how do you do it?" She would just smile and say, "Oh, honey, I don't have a secret. It's just all about having good dirt."

Are you cultivating a good-dirt heart? Jesus says it's the only way to produce a crop.

THERE'S NO PLACE LIKE HOME:
The Prodigal Son

LUKE 15:11–32

*Home is the place where, when you have
to go there, they have to take you in.*

—Robert Frost

Have you ever lost your way home? I remember getting lost in a dangerous area of a large city and trying to find my way back to the interstate. I kept driving around and around the same area. Then I had a revelation. My car had a built-in GPS (Global Positioning System), which I love because I'm the most directionally challenged person on this planet. All I had to do was press "home" and the GPS began to instruct me. Within a short time, I was back in familiar territory on the interstate.

Even Einstein Lost His Way

Albert Einstein was a great scientist, famous for the formula $E=mc^2$ (energy equals mass multiplied by the speed of light squared). Einstein was so brilliant that simple things confused him. He was known to be very forgetful. When he had moved to a new home in

143

Princeton, New Jersey, where he taught at the Institute of Advanced Studies of Princeton University, an unusual thing happened.

> The telephone rang one day in the office of the dean of the Princeton Graduate School. The voice at the other end inquired: "May I speak to Dr. Einstein, please?"
>
> The secretary replied, "He's not in today."
>
> The voice continued, "Perhaps you could tell me where Dr. Einstein lives."
>
> The secretary replied, "Oh, no sir, I could never do that because Dr. Einstein wants his privacy respected."
>
> Then the caller's voice dropped to a whisper: "Please don't tell anyone, but I'm Dr. Einstein and I have forgotten how to get home."

It is a terrible feeling to forget how to get home—or even worse, to forget "home" altogether.

📖 What is it about home that makes people want to return?

_____

📖 Is home a place where you feel loved? Why or why not?

_____

📖 Is home a place of acceptance, no matter what you've done? Why or why not?

_____

📖 Is home a place where you feel safe and secure? Why or why not?

_____

Dorothy in *The Wizard of Oz* kept saying, "There's no place like home; there's no place like home." She's right. There is no place like home. Home should be a place we can always come back to, where we are loved and accepted. Jesus teaches that when you come to know the Father, you are always welcomed home, no matter the circumstances.

> *A man travels the world over in search of what he needs and returns home to find it.*
>
> —George Moore

 What Is a Parable?

Parables are rich in symbolism and illustrate profound and divine truths. Jesus used parables to relate common things—lost coins, sheep, a sower's seed—to spiritual truths and applications.

Parables were a common form of teaching in Judaism, so when reading a parable we must always ask, "What did these words mean to the original audience, and what do these words mean to me today?"

As mentioned previously, a parable is similar to an apple. The skin is the story itself, the meat is the context, and the core is the spiritual application.

The Lost Son

The parable of the prodigal son is well known. It has three main characters: The father, the lost son, and the older son. Let us now focus on the father and the lost son. Discussion of the older son is a whole chapter in itself.

> A certain man had two sons. And the younger of them said to his father, "Father, give me the portion of goods that falls to me." So he divided to them his livelihood. And not many days after, the younger son gathered all together, journeyed to a far country, and there wasted his possessions with prodigal living. But when he had spent all, there arose a severe famine in that land, and he began to be in want. Then he went and joined himself to a citizen of that country, and he sent him into his fields to feed swine. And he

would gladly have filled his stomach with the pods that the swine ate, and no one gave him anything (Luke 15:11–16).

Using the apple analogy, consider first the outer layer. A son leaves home, squanders all he has, lives an ungodly life, and returns to his father who accepts him back.

Next, look at the inner layer of the parable. Jewish law provided that a father with two sons leave a double portion (two-thirds) of his estate to the older son at his death, while leaving only one-third to the younger. It was unusual for a father to settle his estate while still living. Since the estate wasn't usually settled until the death of the benefactor, the son's request was a disgrace to his father. The father probably had to sell some of the land or livestock or liquidate his assets to grant his son's request. The amazing part of this parable is that the father granted his son's request.

The father in the parable must have been heartbroken because his son's request indicated that the father had not died soon enough. The son's attitude showed a lack of love and respect for the father. The father, no doubt, shed many tears over his son's foolish behavior.

Consider the Reaction of Jesus' Audience

The audience would have been horrified as Jesus told this parable and at the unreasonable request of the younger son. I can hear the gasp of the audience and see them shaking their heads in disbelief. I can hear them saying to one another, "How can it be? What kind of son would do such a thing?" They also would have wondered, "What kind of father would do this? He should tell his son to leave and never come back because he is so disrespectful."

How do you suppose the father felt at his son's request?

_____

How would you have felt, had you been in the father's place?

You're Free to Go

Here is the core layer of the parable: Jesus was trying to help His audience think spiritually. He wanted them to understand a spiritual truth about His heavenly Father. The father in this parable represents God. Jesus is teaching the extent to which the Father is willing to go to accept us. This parable shows us how deeply the Father loves us.

The lost son in this parable represents the wayward child of God. He knew his father, had a relationship with him, and turned away. He had broken fellowship with his father. We can break fellowship with the Lord as well. We, as Christians, can leave home and go away from Him. Just as in the parable, the boy was still the father's son, but he had left his presence and his favor. Christians can do that as well.

> For it would have been better for them not to have known the way of righteousness, than having known it, to turn from the holy commandment delivered to them (2 Peter 2:21).

When we become Christians, God establishes a love relationship with us. He is always our Father, and He always loves us. No matter how far we go from Him, He remains steadfast, waiting for us to return. But God loves us too much to force obedience or loyalty. He loves us so much that He says, "You're free to go."

The Wrong Concept of God

When the son left home, he "journeyed to a far country" and ended up feeding swine, a task that violated Jewish culture. In today's society, our children and family members sometimes choose activities that are against the teachings of Christ. Many times when Christians leave the faith, they feel as if they cannot come back to God. Too often they develop the idea that He will not accept them because of their mistakes.

Sadly, even those who claim to follow God believe that He is ready to zap them with His magic wand for anything they do wrong. They believe He rejects them completely if they mess up. Those with that belief cannot feel His joy or His love because they live in fear. They believe a vindictive God is ready to grab them and say, "Now I've gotcha! Clean yourself up, get straightened out, come to Me, and then I'll accept you!" One of the reasons people walk away from God instead of repenting is because they have a wrong concept of Him. They feel that God will never accept them because they are too deep in sin. They don't understand who He truly is and what He is really like.

If you have believed this lie about God's rejection of unfaithful children, please understand that Jesus uses the prodigal son to help you comprehend how loving and forgiving the Father is. The truth is, none of us will ever be righteous enough to merit salvation, but because of His perfect Son, we don't have to be.

When we are encouraging prodigals, we often ask, "Don't you believe in God?" But the better question is, "What kind of God do you believe in?" The truth is, it breaks God's heart to see His children suffer from their mistakes. He is for us, not against us. There is nothing that makes the Father more joyful than to see His child come back home to Him. In this parable, Jesus teaches what kind of Father we have—a loving Father who is quick to forgive us.

 ## Coming to Repentance

But the parable doesn't end with the son's staying in the far country. As Luke 15:17 says, "He came to himself." With a renewed spirit, he headed home, hoping his father would allow him to work with the servants in exchange for room and board.

> The Lord is not slack concerning His promise, as some count slackness, but is longsuffering toward us, not willing that any should perish but that all should come to repentance (2 Peter 3:9).

The Father wants us to come to repentance, but He will not force us. Forced obedience and repentance never last because they are not from the heart. God wants our heart. He wants us to love and serve Him with our whole heart.

A mother told her rambunctious little girl to sit down and be quiet. The little girl refused to listen. Finally, the mother told her, "Sit down and be quiet or you are going to get a spanking." The little girl sat down, but had a mean scowl on her face. The mother asked her why she looked so angry. The little girl replied, "I may be sitting down on the outside but I am standing up on the inside." That's inward rebellion, not true repentance.

Repentance means to "turn away from." We don't stay in our sin once we repent of it. In a classroom, I illustrate repentance by holding a card with the word "sin" written on it. Then I lay "sin" down and walk away from it. Many of us fail at repentance because we don't understand what it means. When we truly repent, it is just like the illustration: we walk away from it. We have to become conscious of our sin and understand that we can no longer live in our sin and be pleasing to God. The wayward son in the parable is the perfect example. However, the father never gives up on his son. He never stops loving him.

 ## The Reunion

Notice again the red-letter verses from the text:

> But when he came to himself, he said, "How many of my father's hired servants have bread enough and to spare, and I perish with

hunger! I will arise and go to my father, and will say to him, "Father, I have sinned against heaven and before you, and I am no longer worthy to be called your son. Make me like one of your hired servants" And he arose and came to his father. But when he was still a great way off, his father saw him and had compassion, and ran and fell on his neck and kissed him (Luke 15:17-20).

The son comes to himself; he realizes his sin and foolish behavior. He decides to swallow his pride, give up the thought of eating the pods he was feeding the pigs, and go home. He admits his sin, turns from it, and leaves it behind. He is truly penitent. He understands that being one of his father's hired servants is better than the far-country lifestyle. The son is quick to say, "I have sinned against heaven and you. I am no longer worthy to be called your son." Owning up to our sins is difficult. But when we come to understand that all sin is against God and no one deserves to be saved, we are in a position to understand and accept God's grace.

▌▌ Why do we need to recognize that nothing is better than being a child of the Father?

_____

▌▌ How did the father react (Luke 15:20–23)?

_____

▌▌ What would be a normal parent's reaction?

_____

▌▌ Did the father react with accusations, belittlement, or chastisement? Discuss.

_____

📖 How does the father's looking from a great way off for his son's return comfort you?

_____

These verses give us a clear perspective of God the Father. The boy's father had to be brokenhearted when his son left home. He thought of his son every day. He longed for his return. He, no doubt, often walked to the edge of his property for a better view. Can you imagine how the father must have felt when his son did return? When he saw the familiar figure walking toward him in an unfamiliar manner, maybe he thought, "This can't be my son. He wouldn't be dressed like that; he wouldn't be walking with his head bowed. It just can't be . . ." But it was.

When he realized the boy was his son, he ran to meet him. In the Jewish culture, men wore robes. Running would have required that the father pull up his robe, exposing his legs, a highly undignified act. He didn't care. He raised his robe anyway and ran unashamedly. The father grabbed the boy as he began confessing the enormity of his sins and began kissing him. The Greek meaning behind "the father kissed him" is that he kept on kissing him, smothering him with kisses.

The father didn't start belittling, criticizing, or accusing him. He loved him and welcomed him back home, the place where he belonged all along. What a beautiful red-letter description about our Father's love toward us! Our God is full of love and mercy, and He is always willing to meet us when we return.

📖 How does the father's reaction help explain the love the heavenly Father has for us?

_____

📖 What can you do to stop His love for you?

_____

📖 What can you do to stop His forgiveness of your sins?

📖 What would you say to those who think they have moved too far from God to get them to understand how much the Father wants us to return to Him?

You see, my friend, just as the father clothed his pitiful, smelly, barefooted son at his return, our heavenly Father will do the same for you and me.

Consider the following facts about the father-and-son reunion:

- Since the son didn't think he was worthy, he intended to say to his father, "I'll just be a hired servant; a slave." But the father stopped him when he said, "I'm no longer worthy to be called your son." In essence, the father replied, *No, you are my son. I will cover you with the robe of righteousness.* That robe was one of distinction to set him apart from everyone else.

- The father reestablished his relationship with the son by giving him a new ring, symbolizing full family status and a sign of authority. The ring would have borne the engraved family seal.

- Slaves in that culture didn't wear shoes but sons did. The father put new shoes on his feet.

- The father restored everything the son had lost.

Are You Lost? Go Home!

The key to understanding this parable is found in the first two verses of Luke 15: "Then all the tax collectors and the sinners drew near to Him to hear Him. And the Pharisees and scribes complained, saying, 'This Man receives sinners and eats with them.'" In that culture, having a meal with someone meant that you accepted that person.

A hungry woman was invited to a Bible devotional followed by a meal. After the devotional, she was in the line to receive soup. She mentioned to the preacher that she was ready to obey Jesus. She said, "I never knew my name was in the Bible."

The preacher smiled and said, "What's your name?"

She said, "My name is Edith, and my name is in the Bible."

The preacher said, "I'm sorry ma'am, but you must be mistaken. The name Edith does not appear in the Bible."

She said, "Oh yes, it does. You read it a few minutes ago."

He opened his Bible, and with a dirty finger she pointed to Luke 15:2 and said, "See, there it is. Jesus received sinners and 'Edith' with them."

And indeed He does. The good news is that Jesus does receive Edith . . . and Maggie, Zach, Arvy, Jenna, Anna, and any other sinner who will come to Him.

Remember my telling of being lost in a large city? Experiences like that can help us know that we can be spiritually lost. We can wander away from God in many ways; however, with God we can always push the GPS button and return safely home.

I have a new definition for Global Positioning System: *God's Privilege System.* And *privilege* means: "A special right granted to someone or group."

When children of God realize they are separated from Him by their sin and then turn away from it, they return safely "home" to the Father. That is the beautiful privilege of being the Father's children. And just as the father waited for his prodigal son, our Father will always be waiting for us with open arms. After all, there's no place like home.

PARTING REMARKS

Jesus: The Sweetest Name I Know

We are living at a time when being politically correct is popular. We live in an era when everybody claims the name of God, but nobody wants to say the name "Jesus." We don't want to offend anyone—the Muslims, the Buddhists, the Hindus, the Jews—or anyone who doesn't believe that Jesus came, lived, died, and rose again for the sins of the world. The name of Jesus sets us apart from the religions of the world, because no other religion claims an empty tomb.

> And entering the tomb, they saw a young man clothed in a long white robe sitting on the right side; and they were alarmed. But he said to them, "Do not be alarmed. You seek Jesus of Nazareth, who was crucified. He is risen! He is not here. See the place where they laid Him" (Mark 16:5–6).

The Bible proclaims that there is coming a time when, at the name of Jesus, every knee will bow and every tongue will confess His sweet name.

> Therefore God also has highly exalted Him and given Him the name which is above every name, that at the name of Jesus every knee should bow, of those in heaven, and of those on earth, and of those under the earth, and that every tongue should confess that Jesus Christ is Lord, to the glory of God the Father (Philippians 2:9–11).

There is no way to heaven except through Jesus. Jesus told Thomas, "I am the way, the truth, and the life. No one comes to the Father except through Me" (John 14:6).

When Jesus tells us that He is the way, He distinguishes Himself as the only way. A way is a path or a route that one follows. Jesus tells us there is only one path to the Father and it is through Him.

Jesus emphasizes Himself as "the truth." He is the only truth. In the Sermon on the Mount Jesus repeated "But I say to you . . . " (Matthew 5:22, 28, 32, 34, 44), equating Himself as the authoritative standard of righteousness. Jesus was the incarnate Word of God, and He is the source of all truth. "In the beginning was the Word, and the Word was with God, and the Word was God" (John 1:1).

Jesus declared that He is the life. John explained, "In Him was life, and the life was the light of men" (John 1:4). Jesus promised to lay down His life for His sheep and then to take it up again (John 10:17–18). He promised His followers, "Because I live, you will live also" (John 14:19). As His children, we will live forever.

Since Jesus is life, we can have deliverance from a life of sin and bondage in this life: "I have come that they may have life, and that they may have it more abundantly" (John 10:10).

Jesus assured us that He would give peace to His followers and that He would leave that peace with them: "Peace I leave with you, My peace I give to you; not as the world gives do I give to you. Let not your heart be troubled, neither let it be afraid" (John 14:27).

It is through Jesus that we have salvation. "Nor is there salvation in any other, for there is no other name under heaven given among men by which we must be saved" (Acts 4:12).

No wonder there is no sweeter name than Jesus.

- He is the way, the truth, and the life.

- He came to give us a better life while we live upon the earth, and He gave us His peace.

- He assured us that we would live eternally because He lives.

- His name is the sweetest name because there is no other name by which we can be saved.

- His name is even sweeter, because He gave Himself so that He might bring us to God, and make us alive by His Spirit (1 Peter 3:18).

In ancient days, students followed closely behind their rabbi. The dust of their rabbi's feet, as they moved through the countryside, covered them because they followed so closely. They didn't want to miss anything the rabbi said or taught. The custom was "to be covered in the dust of your rabbi."

It is my prayer that this book will help you to be covered in the dust of your Rabbi, Jesus. I pray that you come to know and believe there is no sweeter name than His. You will discover there is no one like Him by reading His words in the red letters. He will get even sweeter as the days go by. Familiarize yourself so much with the life of Jesus that you begin to think like Him, act like Him, and be like Him.

Read the Gospels often. Follow the reading schedule on the next page. Make it a priority to read through the Gospels several times a year, as I have come to practice in my faith. That habit is life changing. Let every day be "A Red-Letter Day."

—Debbie Dupuy

FORTY-DAY CHALLENGE:
Reading Schedule for the Gospels

It's a red-letter day! Since we are studying the life and words of Jesus, why not read the biographies of Jesus together? Let's do it. Then we'll celebrate!

1 Make a commitment to read daily.

2 Set aside a specific time each day. Set your schedule and then stick to it. Mornings are great, but feel free to use any time that works consistently for you. (You can download a Bible app free on your iPhone.)

3 Read the Bible for the sake of learning, not simply to fulfill your commitment. Pray before you begin, asking God to give you wisdom and understanding, and then be refreshed by the words you read. Record what you learn about Jesus in your notebook.

Date to be finished:

Day 1—Matthew 1; Matthew 2

Day 2—Matthew 3; Matthew 4

Day 3—Matthew 5; Matthew 6

Day 4—Matthew 7; Matthew 8

Day 5—Matthew 9; Matthew 10

Day 6—Matthew 11; Matthew 12

Day 7—Matthew 13; Matthew 14

Day 8—Matthew 15; Matthew 16

Day 9—Matthew 17; Matthew 18

Day 10—Matthew 19; Matthew 20

Day 11—Matthew 21; Matthew 22

Day 12—Matthew 23; Matthew 24

Day 13—Matthew 25; Matthew 26

Day 14—Matthew 27; Matthew 28

Day 15—Mark 1; Mark 2

Day 16—Mark 3; Mark 4

Day 17—Mark 5; Mark 6

Day 18—Mark 7; Mark 8

Day 19—Mark 9; Mark 10

Day 20—Mark 11; Mark 12

Day 21—Mark 13; Mark 14

Day 22—Mark 15; Mark 16

Day 23—Luke 1; Luke 2

Day 24—Luke 3; Luke 4

Day 25—Luke 5; Luke 6

Day 26—Luke 7; Luke 8

Day 27—Luke 9; Luke 10

Day 28—Luke 11; Luke 12

Day 29—Luke 13; Luke 14

Day 30—Luke 15; Luke 16

Day 31—Luke 17; Luke 18

Day 32—Luke 19; Luke 20; Luke 21

Day 33—Luke 22; Luke 23; Luke 24

Day 34—John 1; John 2; John 3

Day 35—John 4; John 5; John 6

Day 36—John 7; John 8; John 9

Day 37—John 10; John 11; John 12; John 13

Day 38—John 14; John 15; John 16

Day 39—John 17; John 18; John 19

Day 40—John 20; John 21

ENDNOTES

1 Louis Klopsch, "Explanatory Note" in *The Holy Bible: Red Letter Edition* (New York: Christian Herald, 1901), p. xvi. As cited in "The Origins of the Red-Letter Bible" (March 23, 2006). https://www.crossway.org /articles/red-letter-origin. Access date: July 7, 2017.

2 Steve Eng, "The Story Behind: Red Letter Bible Editions," *Bible Collectors' World* (Jan/Mar 1986). http://biblecollectors.org/articles /red_letter_bible.htm.

3 "The Origins of the Red-Letter Bible" (March 23, 2006). https://www .crossway.org/articles/red-letter-origin.

4 Klopsch, "Explanatory Note," p. xvi.

5 Leonard Sweet and Frank Viola, *Jesus: A Theography* (Nashville: Thomas Nelson, 2012), p. 302.

6 Lu Paradise, "What Famous & Infamous People Had to Say About Jesus" (August 25, 2010). https://starrynews.wordpress.com/2016 /02/04/what-famous-infamous-people-had-to-say-about-jesus.

7 "Death of the Apostles." https://bible.org/illustration/death-apostles.

8 Wayne Jackson, "Nero Caesar and the Christian Faith," Christian Courier.com. https://www.christiancourier.com/articles/623-nero -caesar-and-the-christian-faith. Access date: February 8, 2017.

9 Mark Galli and Ted Olsen, eds., *131 Christians Everyone Should Know* (Nashville: Broadman and Holman, 2000), p. 361.

10 David Platt, *Radical: Taking Back Your Faith from the American Dream* (Colorado Springs: Multnomah, 2010), p. 181.

11 "Year-in-Review: Barna's Top 10 Findings from 2014" (Dec. 30, 2014), Barna.com. https://www.barna.com/research/year-in-review-barnas -top-10-findings-from-2014.

12 "We Reap What We Sow," *Michael* (Oct. 1, 2002). http://www.michael journal.org/articles/terrorism-revolutions/item/we-reap-what-we-sow? /reap.htm. Access date: July 7, 2017.

13 Kat Eschner, "'9-1-1' Has Meant 'Help, Please' for 49 Years," Smithsonian.com (February 16, 2017). http://www.smithsonianmag .com/smart-news/9-1-1-has-meant-help-please-49-years-180962143.

14 F. F. Bruce, *New International Bible Commentary* (Grand Rapids: Zondervan, 1979), p. 1124.

15 David Alexander, *1937 Eerdmans' Handbook to the Bible* (Grand Rapids: Eerdmans, 1973), p. 478.

16 Bob Bennett, words & music. "Man of the Tombs." (Matters of the Heart Music, 1989) (ASCAP). Used by permission. www.bobbennett .com.

17 Bruce, *New International Bible Commentary*, p. 1124.

18 "Year-in-Review," Barna.com.

19 Christianity Stack Exchange.com, March 26, 2013. http://christianity .stackexchange.com/questions/14762/why-did-jesus-not-want-people -to-talk-about-his-healing. Access date: May 14, 2017.

20 Sweet, *Jesus: A Theography*, pp. 167–169.

21 Robert E. Webber, *Ancient-Future Worship: Proclaiming and Enacting God's Narrative* (Grand Rapids: Baker, 2008), p. 34.